The Teaching of Literature
with special reference to developing
countries

H. L. B. Moody

LONGMAN

LONGMAN GROUP LTD
London

*Associated companies, branches and representatives
throughout the world*

© Longman Group Ltd 1971

First published 1971
New impressions*1972; *1976; *1977

ISBN 0 582 52602 7

*Printed in Hong Kong by
Yu Luen Offset Printing Factory Ltd*

Contents

Acknowledgements

We are grateful to the following for permission to reproduce extracts from their work:

A. N. Whitehead, *The Aims of Education*; Joseph Conrad, *Victory*; Muriel Spark, *The Go Away Bird*; Ezekiel Mphahlele, *Down Second Avenue*; Grahame Green, *The Comedians*; J. S. Bruner, *Towards a Theory of Instruction*; Robert Bolt, *A Man for All Seasons*; T. Stoppard, *Rosencrantz and Guildenstern are Dead*; Edward Sapir, *Language*; Sam Tulya-Muhika, *Short East African Plays in English*; S. H. Burton, *A Pageant of Longer Poems*

1

What *is* Literature?

This is not a question which is likely to cause much trouble to those who are likely to be reading this book. Literature, in one form or another touches the lives of all educated people at some stage and there can surely be little mystery about what it *is*. Nevertheless it is an excellent thing for all who are concerned with any particular form of study, whether as teachers or as students, to think out clearly what it is essentially concerned with. In so doing, they will be able to convince both themselves and others that they are not just slavishly following an antiquated tradition but are engaging themselves in something which is clearly reasonable, useful – perhaps even indispensable!

Those who are of a philosophical turn of mind may like to follow the discussion of what Literature is into the realms of abstract speculation, in a book such as Wellek and Warren's *The Theory of Literature*. Here we shall approach the problem in a practical way. The word 'literature' can be found in a number of different kinds of statement, and this suggests that Literature is in fact not the name of a simple, straightforward phenomenon, but an 'umbrella' term which covers a number of different kinds of activity. We can talk of Literature in general, for example, as a branch of human activity distinct from Agriculture or Science, without consideration of culture, race, or nation – as something which certain people in every community throughout the world have exerted themselves to produce and which others in even greater numbers have striven to 'consume', whether by listening personally or by the reading of manuscripts, pamphlets, magazines or printed books. We also talk of Literature as something associated with, and characteristic of, a particular nation, or people, or groups of people; for example, Arabic Literature, American Literature, Commonwealth Literature, West Indian Literature, African Literature and so on; and in such cases Literature obviously has some kind of collective significance, transcending the particular individuals who produce and consume it. Then again we can talk of the Literature of a particular historical period or movement, which may often be cross-cultural, i.e. it may be found in the Literature of a number of different cultures; for example, Renascence Literature, Romantic Literature, Surrealist Literature, Twentieth-century Literature, Colonial Literature, the Literature of Independent Africa, and so on. In a rather different way we can talk of the literature of a particular subject or topic, e.g. the literature of ship-building, of child development, even the literature of linguistics, and in this sense, of course, we mean everything of significance that has ever been written about that subject. Last but not least, if much of our time has been spent in institutions of education, we may think of Literature as a subject in the school or college timetable, distinctly different from Biology, History or Physical Education; and in this connection we shall have an impression that Literature is subdivided into various sub-categories such as Poetry, Fiction, Drama, Satire, Tragedy, and quite a few others.

While Literature, however, often becomes a subject of study, a form of work or of training, we must not forget that it is fundamentally something engaged in, whether by producer or consumer, voluntarily and spontaneously; not only for some immediate pleasure, but because it is found to offer various kinds of highly prized satisfaction which can be obtained in no other way.

So far we have been talking about the various types of Literature. The question remains: What *is* Literature? What, for example, is its 'raw material'? And the answer, which we can hardly escape, and which fits everyone of the species and varieties we have just reviewed is, in every case – Language! Language either spoken, or written. If we can say that Literature is Language, perhaps we should be rather more precise and say that Literature consists of certain rather specialized forms, selections and collections of Language. There is not a single community of human beings on the face of this earth which does not possess its own 'language' – by language we mean those distinctive speech sounds which are used in various kinds of systematic pattern to communicate all the messages necessary for the smooth running and well-being of the community ('conventionally patterned noise contextualized' as it has been summed up in four words). All language of course is based on forms of speech, but most languages have developed systems for recording language in more permanent, written forms.

Now, language as a means of social communication and control, of course, includes a whole variety of utilitarian functions which we hardly think of as 'literary'. Every language is used countless times each day for such useful and necessary things as greetings, enquiries, instructions, information, news, reports, proposals, contracts, and so on; and these we should rarely be inclined to include in the categories of Literature. Language, then, involves a wider range of activity and references than Literature; indeed, our conception of Language must include absolutely every kind of communication which involves the use of symbols based on speech. Literature occupies a territory of some size and importance within the total realm of Language, but not the whole field: a person (e.g. a lawyer) may be much concerned with some of the uses of language without being at all in contact with Literature; on the other hand anyone who is concerned with Literature will be compelled to remember at many points that basically he is concerned with Language. If we attempt to represent the relationship diagrammatically, it would perhaps be something like Fig. 1, on page 3.

Here the outer circle represents the whole realm of language, subdivided into various areas of function and occasion, while the inner meandering shape represents the fields of literature, playing a more important part in some areas (e.g. social relationships) than in others (e.g. scientific research). On second thoughts, we may feel that this diagram does not represent all aspects of relationship between Language and Literature, and perhaps Fig. 2 would be nearer the whole truth, for we should remember that the activities of creative writers at various times and in various ways extend the boundaries of language, and invent new forms and uses of the language which the whole community in time comes to employ.

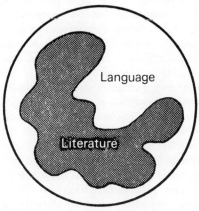

Fig. 1

Having accepted the fact that all Literature is constructed out of Language, we can now go further into the nature of Literature. A work of literature is, of course, something *more* than the language from which it is constructed. As the function of language is to make references to the experiences of the people who use it, so works of literature must be regarded as highly complex, elaborated statements about the world of the writer and his readers.

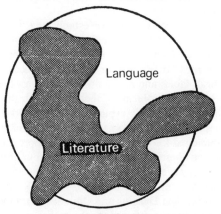

Fig. 2

In the early stages of a culture, it is rarely possible to learn much about individual authors: the production of literature has then more often been a process of communal or folk creation, in which many individuals have collaborated to hand on traditional myths, stories and songs, fresh details being added or changed at various times without the character of the whole being greatly altered. In more recent centuries, as the human appetite for exact facts and records has become greater, we tend to know a good deal more about authors who produce literature (as the back cover of any Penguin novel illustrates). Writers tend, too, in later ages, to be a good deal more independent and individual, expressing their own personal point of view, rather than a collective one. Nevertheless, they sometimes make use of traditional material for contemporary purpose; for example, the use by W. H. Auden of the mediaeval ballad form, the adaptation of Jean Anouilh of ancient Greek myths and tragedies, James Thurber's modification of the ancient animal fables, and modern African dramatists' use of traditional themes. Literature, we observe, seems to undergo a kind of evolution along with other features of the culture it belongs to, though as in other kinds of evolutionary growth the basic archetypal patterns can often be clearly traced in later developments.

It is perhaps helpful to distinguish three very fundamental areas of human life, upon which, from earlier times up to the present day, literature has been particularly centred. These are the religious, the social, and the personal. The religious impulse is seen in its earliest forms in expressions of prayer and praise, often accompanying ritual, to whatever Gods were recognized, with the idea of gaining their approval, their help, or their mercy. At later stages it was – and of course still is – expressed in works of 'devotion', inspired by the more developed doctrines of the great world religions (Buddhism, Christianity, Hinduism, Islam, etc.). Even in the modern, more secularized world the religious impulse can be seen in all those works, in whatever category, which attempt to express man's perception of the creation he is a part of, his destiny in that creation, and his attitude towards it. Samuel Becket's *Waiting for Godot*, for example, can be described as one of the great religious dramas of the present century.

The social impulse is concerned with establishing, and maintaining, the kinds of behaviour and relationship between individuals, and between the individual and the community, which are necessary for the greatest well-being of all concerned. In earliest times this produced a vast variety of 'animal' and 'moral' fables and is still producing a vast literature concerned with the ethical ideas and problems of modern man in the modern world.

The third impulse, towards the exploration of the personal, can be traced back to the stories of heroic ancestors who founded communities, established institutions, championed freedom, and overcame oppressors. By a long process of development, these became modified into our modern biographies, and autobiographies; novels, dramas and poems concerned with good men, bad men, and ordinary men (and women) – from King Lear to Madame Bovary, and on to Stephen Dedalus and Odili Samalu, in which writers have tried to explore and sometimes to change the nature of human consciousness.

After all these generalizations, it is important to stress that the greater part of our satisfaction in literature comes from our acquaintance with, and appreciation of, individual works. It is more important to have enjoyed a number of individual works than to arrive at the most grandiose of generalizations which have no basis in personal experience and appreciation.

In the modern world, literary writers have become very prolific; and, while some of the literary outpouring may at times seem trivial, ephemeral, wasteful, the general honour and respect which Literature as an art form receives, is probably as high as ever. We are accustomed to hearing our modern world (especially so-called Western Civilization) condemned for being excessively technological and materialistic. It is difficult to accept this, especially as we gain some acquaintance with the achievements of modern literature, and understand how it reflects the great concern of modern man not only for the outward circumstances, but also for the essential conditions of his existence.

2

Literature in Education

Using the demand for English to impose literary studies is a very unwise policy. –
Bruce Pattison.

We may begin by taking note of Professor Pattison's warning, and ask why it
is necessary. Two facts are very clear:
1. In many parts of the world today there is a strong demand for English as
   a language of international communication, of business and commerce,
   and of higher education.
2. In the past there has been a tendency to meet this demand by offering (or
   'imposing') traditional types of English course centred upon the literary
   classics of the language (Chaucer, Shakespeare, Milton, and Dickens, etc.)
   without much thought as to how such studies are of use.
The discrepancy between these facts has led more recently to a reform of
English teaching, giving much greater attention to the language, and literary
studies have as it were been quietly pushed into the shade. As is the case with
many reforms, the pendulum has perhaps swung too far from one extreme to
the other, and our principal concern in this book is to consider in a rational
way what the place of literary studies ought to be in the educational curriculum
of developing societies, and more particularly what *kind* of literary studies
should be offered.

Of course, if works of literature were of no use in interpreting and dealing
with the world of reality, there would be no very good reason for spending
much time on them, whether in developing or in any other societies. If, however, it can be shown that works of literature, or even a certain selection of
them, can have a relevance to these problems of reality, then we must certainly
consider them as of some importance. It is in the conviction that literary
studies, rightly undertaken, can make an important contribution in developing
societies which are faced with many stubbornly realistic problems, that this
book has been written.

Let us consider what are the needs of developing societies which education
can help to meet. A great deal has been written and spoken on this topic, and
we can conveniently summarize it all by saying that the welfare and progress
of such societies must be based on development of two kinds – individual and
collective. They will be able to achieve their aims only if individual members
acquire the *skills*, the *knowledge*, and qualities of personal *character* needed to
deal with the problems, techniques and opportunities of the modern world.
But individuals will only be able to put these qualities to full use if the com-

munities they live and work in embody qualities of *harmony, efficiency,* and *flexibility.* Some of these things (e.g. repairing a car) can be taught quite quickly and permanently; others (e.g. raising a national revenue) are much more complex, and depend not only on specific techniques, but on the energy, imagination, integrity – and ultimately the underlying values and beliefs, of the individuals concerned, especially those who are in privileged or responsible positions.

To be realistic we must admit that few of these desirable things can be produced solely by education in institutions (schools, colleges, polytechnics, and so on); other agencies such as governments, business houses, religious organizations, journalists, writers, entertainers, and public leaders exercise a tremendous influence also. Nevertheless it is in its educational institutions that a community attempts to define its objectives, and schools and colleges must certainly be oriented towards what is regarded as valuable for the community.

How, within the total field of education, can the study of literature make its maximum contribution? Provided that the precautions suggested in the rest of this book (and especially in Chapter 3) are observed, the study of literature can help in the following ways.

1 Skills

We have already touched upon the close relationship between Literature and Language. Language skills are of four types: those involved in (i) listening (ii) speaking (iii) reading (iv) writing. The inclusion of literature in the curriculum helps to train students in the skill of reading, and perhaps a little in listening, speaking and writing. A student listens to literature read aloud by the teacher (or on records or tapes) and to the discussions that literature always stimulates in the class. He speaks when he acts in plays, when he reads poems and when he takes an active part in discussions. Because literature is interesting, he wants to talk about it. It can provide plenty of interesting opportunities for writing too.

2 Knowledge

Literature does not of course concentrate on a particular area of knowledge, as for example does Chemistry or History. Literature, we can say with some reason, is concerned with all aspects of man and the universe in their entirety. Certainly every work of literature is about *something,* often about many things; and the more a person reads, the better stocked will his mind be with knowledge. Knowledge, of course, is a complex conception; we can analyse it, and the way it is acquired from literature, in a number of ways. There are, for example, the facts that are actually encountered and explained in the work of literature; there are also the facts that we are impelled to discover from other sources in order to understand particular situations or problems that occur in literature. Sooner or later, students come to the realization that separate 'facts' in themselves are less important than the ways in which they support and illustrate each other. Most important of all is the realization, which comes to all sooner or later, that the facts worth knowing are not only facts about 'things', but the facts about life. The facts about life include not only the answers to the questions: 'Who's Who?' and 'Who did What?', but also all the answers to such questions as: What are human beings like? What can be expected of them? Why do they behave as they do? How do they get on together? What is my own aim in life?

While it would be foolish to claim that literature has all the answers to all these questions, it may safely be claimed that it has quite a few. Most important of all, perhaps, it can stimulate its students to *ask relevant questions*, so that they are more likely to arrive at a true understanding of the problems, whether by the reading of literature or by other methods of investigation.

A special kind of knowledge which every society must foster is that concerning its own culture. The word 'culture' is used lavishly nowadays, with many different meanings and implications. Here we use it to signify what is peculiarly characteristic of a particular community, including its organization, institutions, laws, customs, work, play, art, religion and so on – its 'totality'. It is important in any system of education to impart to each individual a comprehensive insight into his own culture, for this gives him pride, self-confidence, and a sense of belonging. Some of this knowledge is transmitted in the family, in places of worship; and some in various parts of the school curriculum. Literature, however, can often fill in any gaps and weld the whole into a meaningful picture.

Nowadays we live more and more in one world, a 'global village' as it has been called – and this remains true regardless of various political divisions. Improved communications are helping us to develop an international culture, and one of the tasks of education is to acquaint us with the widest range of human achievements without destroying pride in our indigenous culture. For example, an educated European may legitimately be expected to know something of the technical achievements of U.S.A., the sculptures of West Africa, the music and dancing of Russia, the great religions of the East; an educated African or Asian may be expected to know something of the literature of America, the art of the Mediterranean countries, the political institutions of Britain, the social organization of China, and so on. Studies in Literature, if wisely undertaken, will bring us into contact with some of the world's great minds and personalities, the great teachers and thinkers of all ages. We could manage to live without knowledge of such things and such people, but having made their acquaintance, we could not wish to be without them. Without some acquaintance with the total field of human culture, we should often find ourselves baffled by what other people are talking and writing about. A glance at any piece of unspecialized discourse (e.g. a great international newspaper or magazine) quickly shows us how educated people are able to refer to a wide background of culture as an essential element in their thinking and communication.

3 Development

We cannot for long think of education only in terms of abstracts like Skill and Knowledge, for, as every teacher must be aware, every student is an individual, with his own particular personality, his own abilities, his own problems, his own rate of development. It is important therefore to see the whole of education as a process of development in the individual. Yet while the individual is, as the word suggests, a complex unity, it is possible to see in him a number of different 'faculties', for some of these can at times be underdeveloped or over-developed; they all, however, must be developed in harmony if he is to realize his fullest potential and make the most useful contribution to the affairs of his generation. The principal faculties to be trained are the *sensory* (or *sensori-motor*), the *intellectual*, the *affective* (the *'feelings'*), the *social* and, some would certainly add, the religious sense. For each of these, literature can provide suitable materials and encouragement. It can be argued, too, that better than any other subject, literature provides opportunities for the development of *all* these faculties in relation to each other, which comes very near to the aim of the fullest education.

(a) *The senses.* The study of literature can be used to extend the range of perceptions of all the classic senses, of sight, hearing, taste, scent and touch. Many writers have themselves been men of sensitiveness and refinement, who have sought to convey their understanding to the rest of mankind. Following their insights and interpreting the words they have used, the student will be led to recognize an ever-extending range of perceptions and distinctions, as for example between *yellow* and *golden*; *loud* and *stirring*; *fragrant* and *odorous*, and countless others.

Further, as we nowadays acknowledge by the introduction of the term *'sensori-motor'*, we think also of many different kinds of physical activity in which the human body can be trained to express itself; here, too, it will be seen, especially in the field of drama, literature can make a fundamental contribution (see Chapter 7, pages 69–70).

(b) *The intellect.* The training of the intellect is often thought to be the special realm of non-literary subjects (such as mathematics and science). This is a view that should be strenuously challenged. While it is true that those subjects demand strictly controlled, intellectual and logical procedures, it is not those subjects alone which require or permit the use of such procedures. There is the very greatest need in the world today (in developing societies as much as others) for the application of logical and rational methods to vast ranges of non-scientific problems and in those fields the study of literature, if rightly guided, can provide an excellent training. The operation of the rational faculties as opposed to such alternatives as guesswork, impulse, habit, custom, can be as well illustrated and practised in the study of literature as in any other field. The logical process depends on such things as accurate perception, precise interpretation of language, the grouping and classification of data, the drawing of correct inductions and deductions, judgments of various kinds, and the formulation of appropriate courses of action. No student on entering a secondary school is expected to confront all these weighty responsibilities. From the very beginning, however, teachers of literature can encourage respect for facts, distinguishing between what is certain and what is conjectural, establishing the evidence for an opinion, recognizing fallacious methods of argument, and so on.

The idea of intellectual or academic discipline is often encountered, and this seems the place to consider what this means, and the extent to which literary studies can constitute a discipline. 'Discipline' is not primarily a matter of being made to do something unpleasant (as some students might suppose). It is concerned with learning to do something in accordance with a body of well-established rules or standards. An educational system must provide opportunities for free expression, exploration and initiative; but there is another side to human life in which there is little room for free activity and where men must learn to operate within fixed limits which often seem to constrict them.

The whole history, and the future, of the human race depends on man's ability to overcome the stubborn factors in his environment (and in himself). So, from the earliest times the most valued forms of educational discipline have been those which require the student to learn to solve problems, how to 'get things right', and which enable him to *test* the degree of his success. In mathematics, for example, it is easy to check whether a calculation has been carried out correctly; in the study of languages (especially classical languages, such as Latin or Arabic, the rules of which have been finally formulated), it is easy to judge whether a translation has been done in accordance with the rules. In a discipline such as Engineering, there are many stages of inter-mediate testing to ensure that the traffic passes over the new bridge without its collapsing!

How does the study of literature stand in relation to this concept of discipline? Is it just a go-as-you-please subject? – read what you like, think what you like, say what you like! Or has it a discipline of its own? Perhaps the answer will be clear by the time the reader has reached the end of this book!

(c) *The feelings.* The 'culture of the feelings', the 'training of the emotions', is more frequently associated with the study of literature and perhaps needs little defence. Yet even those who believe in it, do not always make clear what they mean by it. While there are many phenomena in human life which can best be dealt with by rational procedures (Shall I go by train or bus? Shall I do this now or next year? etc.), there are also those which, over and above intellectual recognition, demand some kind of emotional response. For example the sight of a grown man beating a small boy seems to demand our indignation, whereas the sight of the sea breaking upon a rocky coast demands our awe and admiration; and we should say that any one who failed to make the normal response was 'less than human'. What exactly 'the emotions' are is not easy to explain. Although they are derived from the basic human instincts, as human institutions have become more complex, they have become attached to things which are more peculiar to each culture (e.g. a baby or a small child evokes admiration throughout the world; but Beethoven's *Missa Solemnis* may seem boring to an educated African, while the tribal tattooings of a Polynesian islander may seem ugly to a European). In some cases, we say that people should 'have some feeling'; at other times, we say that 'feelings need controlling'. Certainly feelings are a very complex and intricate element in human behaviour. To a large extent, any society is concerned with the training of the feelings of its members, inducing people to like what they ought to like, and discouraging them from liking what they ought not to like. While there is usually considerable agreement as to what should be liked or disliked, it is not always possible in all cases to be absolutely definite (e.g. it is wrong to kill, but is it wrong to train men as soldiers?), which probably reflects some of the peculiar moral complications of the human predicament.

Perhaps the most definite thing we can say in this connection is that literature certainly presents us with a wide range of situations and predicaments which seem to stimulate some kind of emotional response; and also that on the whole the writers of literature present those situations in ways which enable us to explore and develop our feelings in an appropriate humane way.

(*d*) *Social awareness.* A newly born infant has no conception of the world apart from its own needs, and all its activities are directed towards the satisfaction of its egocentric requirements. The process of growing up for the human individual is a very long one, especially where it is concerned with the recognition and appreciation of other people; and, of course, this is often quite a painful process, involving conflicts, clashes, and friction of many kinds. A successfully educated person is one who has achieved an attitude of respect towards all the other people in the world, which includes at first his own family, his own friends, his own village, his own tribe; but then beyond that, all the other tribes, nations, and races he may encounter in the world. A mature attitude is based on understanding and interest, and expresses itself in tolerance and friendliness. To be effective, this understanding must embrace all aspects of the ways of other people, including their work, their behaviour, their customs, their religion, and so on.

Effective understanding of other people can only be based on understanding and appreciation of oneself and of one's own culture. The readiness of many members of developing societies in the earlier part of the present century to despise all their own traditions in the pursuit of Europeanization, for example, represented a stage of immature development, comparable to that perhaps of the modern beatniks who wish to ignore all the achievements of their own culture and return to the 'law of the grazing fields'.

There are other subjects in the usual curriculum (we think of history, geography, and the social sciences), which provide valuable education in social awareness. But here again the resources of Literature are an invaluable supplement all along the line. Most imaginative writers, as such, are people who have great capacity for identifying themselves with other people, for putting themselves into other people's positions, for seeing into the heart of a problem; and a teacher of literature, by making a judicious selection, can do a tremendous amount to help his students understand other people, and in the process themselves also.

It is perhaps worth making a special plea, here, to ensure that literature is used to produce a *comprehensive* awareness of other people. Modern writers have done much to stimulate interest in and sympathy for the problems of the unfortunate, the oppressed, the unsuccessful, the deranged, the offender against society, those who need to protest; they are perhaps less inclined to give an equal insight into the problems of those who have to bear difficult responsibilities, to maintain established institutions, and to carry on with the world's unspectacular work.

(*e*) *The religious sense.* This may not at first appear a topic on which many busy people will wish to spend much time. Others find that they can understand and manage their daily life only if their thoughts and actions are based on some underlying system of beliefs. These may be thought of in many different ways, involving orthodox religious concepts, or other kinds of philosophical doctrine. It is true enough that whether we like it or not, whether we *know* it or not, all our thoughts and actions are based on some assumptions, and intelligent human beings will wish to base their lives on better rather than on worse foundations. All we need to add is that teachers who see the need for the exploration of fundamental questions will find abundant material in the realms of literature, for most imaginative writers have been extremely interested in such problems. However students should not assume that every author is in possession of 'the whole truth, and nothing but the truth'. Some authors argue passionately for certain beliefs: others are more concerned with attacking and reforming: always there is a need for the critical assessment of what any particular author seems to be advocating.

4 Character

A well-educated person may have acquired many skills, accumulated much knowledge, undergone whole cycles of individual development, and yet be no very great blessing either to himself or to his fellow men. The 'something more' that is required is usually referred to under the concept of 'character'. As teachers of literature, we must beware of facile assumptions such as that a person who has read a lot of literature is bound to be 'good', while one who hasn't is likely to be 'bad'. It was aptly pointed out at a recent conference that Hitler's Nazi Propaganda Minister, Dr Goebbels, had even taken his Ph.D. in literature! Obviously whether a person ultimately seems to be good or bad is determined by factors very deep in his personality, and there can never be any guarantee that any particular type of education (if we exclude the techniques of brain-washing) will produce any particular result. No form of humane education can 'absolutely determine'; it can only 'seek to shape'.

Nevertheless, two claims can be made for the educational value of literary studies in relation to character. Firstly, the study of literature is likely to develop a keener sense of values in those who gain an intimate acquaintance with it. More than most other kinds of study, it acquaints us with the whole range of possibilities of human life: from happiness, achievement, ecstasy, joy, love, freedom, friendship, self-respect; to greed, defeat, despair, apathy, hate, disintegration, death. A person who has 'been through' the reading of a number of works of literature is likely to have a better sense of what is worthwhile and what is not. The general probability is also that he will thereafter look upon the complexities of life with much greater understanding, insight, tolerance and sympathy – these again are qualities needed in developing societies no less than elsewhere.

The second claim that can be made for the character-training possibilities of literary studies is that they can contribute to the development of that complex of personal qualities which include such things as perseverance, resourcefulness, imagination and creativity. Literature, as we have seen, presents an almost unlimited field of experience. In some kinds of study, the student soon learns what to expect and the methods to be used to solve various problems. Literature, by its nature so various, confronts the student with the opportunity of dealing with an endless stream of fresh and unpredictable experiences. It is thus an excellent preparation for later life, especially at the more professional levels where the educated man has to be ready to take on, evaluate, and make decisions about a wide range of diverse problems. Consider, for example, the doctor in his consulting room, the lawyer in his office, the editor at his desk, the priest in his vestry, or the civil servant with his daily mail: each of them is likely to be concerned with a series of situations which are first of all presented in the form of a verbal statement, whether oral or written.

3

Selection

The previous chapter may have made such extensive claims for the educational value of literary studies that the sceptical reader cannot but recall some literature lessons he may have experienced (whether as teacher or student) which seemed very far from overflowing with such benefits! He may also be able to recall the notable words of Alfred North Whitehead who some years ago launched an attack on the lack of 'vitality in the modern curriculum' in the following scathing terms:

> Algebra, from which nothing follows; Geometry, from which nothing follows; Science, from which nothing follows; History from which nothing follows; a couple of Languages, never mastered; and lastly most dreary of all, Literature, represented by plays of Shakespeare with philological notes and short analyses of plot and character to be in substance committed to memory....

> *(Aims of Education,* 1929)

Whitehead, of course, puts his finger on a vital point: any subject or study 'from which nothing follows', i.e. which has no application to life outside the classroom, is obviously a failure. 'There is only one subject for education', he says, 'and that is Life in all its manifestations'.

It is salutary always for teachers (of any subject) to keep these words in mind as they go about their tasks, if only as a reminder to them to be able to point out what does follow from the work they undertake in the classroom, and how it does apply to 'Life in all its manifestations'. Few teachers would agree that Whitehead's attack is necessarily true of any subject, if rightly envisaged and sensibly taught. Indeed the whole aim of this book is to suggest how literary studies can avoid being the dreary kind of routine for which there is no room in any modern curriculum.

How do we apply Whitehead's warning to the teaching of literature? Let us take a broad view of what we are trying to do. On the one hand we have the huge numbers of the younger generations of mankind hopefully pressing on under the guidance of their elders towards their future and their maturity. On the other hand we have the vast stocks of experience and wisdom, thoughtfully digested and vividly recorded, in the literatures of the world. How do we bring them into fruitful contact? We may perhaps remember one of the famous (or infamous) methods of teaching people to swim – pushing them in at the deep end; and then reflect that there are more enlightened, intelligent and systematic methods of instruction, which achieve the same or better results, with much greater efficiency and much less distress!

The essential educational principle we are approaching here is that *work must always be related to students' capacity* at any stage. Learning is a lengthy business, proceeding as all trained teachers will be aware from the known to the unknown, from the simple to the complex, and involves the necessity for *grading*. Just as students' capacities can be graded, so also all the works of literature in the world could be graded in terms of their simplicity or complexity, their remoteness or their accessibility: and no great success can be expected unless a due relationship between the two parties is observed. We have probably all read of the occasional genius, such as J. S. Mill, who was reading the works of Greek Philosophers by the time he was 4 years old, but such feats of exceptional individuals provide no pattern for the organization of studies for ordinary people. Experienced teachers of literature will have many memories illustrating the need for grading: the poem which provides enormous delight to children of 8/9 years will seem childish to those of 11/12; the novel which may enthral students of 15/16 will be described as boring by those of 12/13. The human animal seems to have various self-protective powers, and fortunately no student can ever be induced to experience enjoyment of a literary experience beyond his range, no matter how great the reputation of the author in adult literary circles!

How, then, is the teacher to set about the selection of literature for his students of various ages in the light of this principle of *grading*? In many actual teaching situations teachers will not be entirely free agents. Their ability to select books will be limited by various factors, such as what is available in the book-store or the local bookshop, syllabuses imposed by higher authority, and the prescriptions of Examination Councils. It may be hoped that if higher authorities have been properly chosen in the first place, they are not likely to impose unsuitable choices, but this perhaps may not always be true; and teachers always have the professional duty (and privilege) of making representations to those authorities outside the classroom which attempt to control their work.

What are the considerations upon which the idea of graded selection must be based? We shall discuss the problem under three aspects which apply equally whether we are considering the teaching of literature in a mother tongue, or in a second or foreign language. We can take note of:

1. Language.
2. Psychology.
3. Background.

1 Language

Mastery of any language is something that grows and expands in each individual by recognizable stages. Similarly works of literature involve many shades of language complexity and sophistication, based not only on the range of subject-matter, but on other factors such as the author's own way of grasping the subjects he deals with, the literary conventions prevailing at the time he is writing, and the kind of readers he assumes himself to be writing for. (Shakespeare, for example, did *not* write his plays to be read by the 'schoolboy . . . with shining morning face, creeping like a snail unwillingly to school'!) To be successful the teacher of literature must develop the knack (or let us say the *skill*) of selecting literature the language of which is in a suitable relation to his students' capacity. When the teaching of language is the first consideration, this is not so difficult nowadays, for most language teaching-courses are automatically provided with linked 'readers' to reinforce the language learning process. This book, however, is more concerned with the wider educational possibilities of literature teaching; we are thinking of students who are past the elementary language-learning stage, when their teachers will need to make their own decisions and choices.

What can the teacher do to check that his selection is linguistically appropriate? It would be possible to set about this with scientific thoroughness, using the techniques being invented nowadays by professional 'linguists', making vocabulary counts, lists of grammatical structures, and so on; and it would probably be useful for every teacher under training to carry out a few such exercises. In practice there is rarely likely to be time for such tests, and in any case the language factor cannot be considered in isolation from the other factors we shall consider. What can be expected is that the teacher should develop an alert sensitiveness to the language capacity of any group of students, and make his selections on that basis.

In estimating the suitability of a text, the teacher must look not only at vocabulary and sentence structures in isolation but at the whole range of concepts and situations which it introduces, and also the accompanying allusions and references. It is important to note the extent to which a writer explains himself as he goes along, or the extent to which he assumes that his readers will be able to follow his allusions without further explanation. Consider the two following opening passages from quite modern authors. Which seems likely to be more fully comprehensible to a secondary school student?:

(*a*) There is, as every schoolboy knows in this scientific age, a very close chemical relation between coal and diamonds. It is the reason, I believe, why some people allude to coal as 'black diamonds'. Both these commodities represent wealth; but coal is a much less portable form of property. There is, from that point of view, a deplorable lack of concentration in coal. Now, if a coalmine could be put in one's waistcoat pocket – but it can't! At the same time, there is a fascination in coal, the supreme commodity of the age in which we are camped like travellers in a garish, unrestful hotel. And I suppose those two considerations, the practical and the mystical, prevented Heyst – Axel Heyst – from going away.

from JOSEPH CONRAD, *Victory*

(b) At Sea Point, on the coast of the Cape of Good Hope, in 1942, there was everywhere the sight of rejoicing, there was the sound of hilarity, and the sea washed up each day one or two bodies of servicemen in all kinds of uniform. The waters round the Cape were heavily mined. The people flocked to bring in the survivors. The girls of the seashore and the harbour waited by twos and threes for the troops on shore leave from ships which had managed to enter the bay safely. I was waiting for a ship to take me to England, and lived on the sea front in the house of Mrs Jan Cloote, a pawnbroker's wife.

from MURIEL SPARK, *The Pawnbroker's Wife*

2 Psychology

Most teachers in training learn something about the psychology of children, and knowledge in this field is as important for the teacher of literature as insight into language. We now appreciate that children are quite different in their psychological make-up from adults, and that they develop through fairly distinct stages. It is essential to be familiar with these stages in choosing works of literature, for they affect such things as students' interests, enthusiasms and aversions; and these in turn affect such things as readiness to co-operate, powers of memory, willingness to make the efforts asked for by the teacher, and the possibility of finding significance in what they are invited to read. The following classification may be regarded with some caution, for psychologists have not established exactly how it applies to children with various cultural backgrounds; nor at what age particular individuals will pass from one stage to another. The boundaries between the stages suggested are not hard and fast, for most students will be ready to go back for a while to earlier stages, though they probably do not have any significant ability to anticipate. Excluding the years of infancy, the principal stages seem to be as follows:

(1) The *autistic* stage (to 8 or 9 years of age). Here children's imaginations are not yet initiated into the world of reality, but delight in many kinds of fantasy.
(2) The *romantic* stage (about 10–12 years of age). This develops out of the previous one and represents a move towards the grasp of reality, but sees the world in highly simplified categories. At this stage, children love stories of heroic exploits, daring adventures, dastardly villains and so on.
(3) The *realistic* stage (about 13–16 years of age). By now children have moved out of the stage of fantasy, and are keenly interested in what *really* happens. 'Is it true?', 'How does he do it?', they wish to know and are ready to follow up avidly the detail which seems to explain the actual affairs of real life.
(4) The *generalizing* stage (from 16 onwards). Now students are not only interested in practical details, but are prepared to abstract, to generalize, to search for the underlying causes of phenomena, to make moral judgements, and generally to 'philosophize'.

Works of literature selected for study should make their appeal at the stage of psychological development which a particular class has reached. In fact, not all members of any class will be at precisely the same stage of development, and the teacher will select works which at least appeal to the majority or average taste.

3 Background

'Background' is the convenient way of referring to the culture which was discussed in Chapter 2 (page 8). Different works may vary considerably in the extent to which an understanding of the background is necessary; but it may include any, or all, of such factors as geography, topography, climate, history, mythology, legends, occupations, institutions, religious and social, personal relationships, habits of thought, social values, moral codes, arts, sports, entertainments, and so on.

In general, students will most easily be attracted to works of literature in which they can quickly recognize a familiar background, preferably with characters somewhat similar to themselves or other people they know. Generally speaking, the teacher will be well advised to apply the principle of working from 'the known to the unknown', and, at least until he has established confident relations with his students, introduce them to literature which does not make excessive demands on their ability to picture what they read.

In the past, students in developing countries have sometimes been plunged into works of literature (and other subjects, e.g. history) in which the whole cultural framework and much of the incidental detail has been unfamiliar. A novel dealing, for example, with the social occasions of eighteenth-century English country gentlemen and their ladies, with much talk of barouches, esplanades, backgammon, spinets, shrubbery walks and Bath Assemblies, etc. might well seem in every sense of the word 'foreign' to inexperienced students. A few unfortunate experiences of this kind might understandably create an aversion for literature altogether, and certainly stimulates the demand which is often heard nowadays for books with local background. This demand is in many ways a very healthy one, firstly because it expresses the expectation that works of literature should relate to life as the student knows it, and secondly as we saw on page 8, because a student should first of all have some appreciation of his own culture before attempting to make contact with other peoples'.

However, teachers will remember that education in its fullest sense is not concerned only with affairs of the 'parish pump'. In a rather familiar phrase, it is concerned with 'opening windows upon the world', and Literature offers one of the best possible ways for people living in one environment to learn something of the lives and problems of people in other parts of the world. The teacher of literature therefore needs to be, in the fullest sense, a 'man of the world', for it is his responsibility to acquire enough knowledge and insight to guide his students through all 'the changing scenes of life' in the works they study.

This is a problem which causes some misgivings amongst teachers who are not certain of their ability to move outside the familiar environments. Teachers are people whose time is very fully occupied, and publishers are beginning to take note of the need for specially prepared editions which give teachers and students much of the help that is needed.

Incidentally, it is often assumed that, because some of the older classics contain difficult expressions and allusions, the more modern the work chosen the easier it will be. This is by no means certain, and there are no short cuts in the process of determining which books are suitable for particular groups of students. Many modern works of literature are just as full of puzzling, contemporary allusions as many of the classics of earlier times.

When students' confidence has been established by the study of some works where they are on familiar ground, they will be very ready to move further afield under the guidance of a teacher they trust. At a secondary school in England known to the present writer some of the most popular books studied at various levels included *Chang, the Elephant Boy* (set in Thailand), *Tell Freedom* (set in South Africa), *Kim* (set in India), *The African Child* (set in Guinea), *Venture to the Interior* (set in Malawi), *Things Fall Apart* (set in Nigeria), and *Catcher in the Rye* (set in America).

Students in developing countries are usually as willing to cross cultural boundaries as English students and, provided that other factors of selection are observed, teachers of literature should plan literature courses that are world-wide in scope.

It does not take long, either, to realize that the apparent difference between 'backgrounds' is often only very superficial; a large range of human problems are in fact almost universal. It was wisely said in Uganda some years ago:

Through the great writers you will inherit more fully the spirit, not of white men, or brown men, or black men, but the spirit that has no colour, the spirit of *man*.

(*Shakespeare in the Tropics*, Inaugural Lecture at Makerere University by ALAN WARNER)

NOTE.
Appendix B gives a suggested list of works of literature set out in graded sequence.

4

A General Approach

In the chapters following this, we shall consider in turn special problems concerned with the teaching of the principal forms of literature. Here, it will be useful, and avoid repetition, to discuss a number of general aspects of the approach to this task. It will become clear that the general principles being considered here are equally relevant to all forms, from the shortest poem to the longest novel. They also all apply equally to work with the most junior class and with the most senior students of a school or college.

The teacher of literature will always work from the twin principles of:
1. Literature as Experience.
2. Literature as Language.

Literature as Experience

The South African writer, Ezekiel Mphahlele, in his autobiography *Down Second Avenue* has an amusing and instructive anecdote of his schooldays, on the occasion of 'reciting poetry':

> We leapt forward to show how 'the Assyrians came down like a wolf on the fold', and stamped on the floor, and I think we drowned our voices ... We understood little of what we were reciting ourselves. Often we asked the teacher to explain some of the lines; he simply said, 'It's poetry, boys and girls, it's poetry, can't you see?' We left it at that, feeling awed.

Now, while there seems to have been some merit in what was going on in that lesson, it was emphatically not characteristic of what a proper literature lesson can, and should, be; above all, because the students *did not understand what they were doing*. In teaching literature, we are not concerned in producing any kind of mechanical, automatic activity, which is meaningless to those who are involved in it. The proper nature of the work can best be grasped by thinking of each particular piece introduced to the students as a new 'experience'. 'Experience' as a whole, of course, means the sum total of all those things that happen to us in the course of our lives, whether things to be enjoyed, to be suffered, to be observed, to be thought about, to initiate, or to co-operate in; experience is traditionally reckoned to make a person more wise, more capable of dealing with further problems. We do not in fact just add together all the experiences we undergo; we assimilate them into our minds and personalities, and organize them eventually into various patterns of classification and expectation, and ultimately our capacity for understanding and acting wisely depends on the range and organization of our stock of experiences. It is obvious that some kinds of experience really happen to us, for example, going on a journey, getting to know a new person, learning a new skill and so on. On the other hand, of almost equal significance are the experiences that come to us from the reading of a poem or a story, or seeing a play.

Experiences may vary in the ease with which they can be assimilated: some are similar to others we have already dealt with and our comment in such cases will be 'Oh yes, that's just like so-and-so . . .'; on other occasions a new experience can be so unexpected, so shattering that it takes us a long time and many uncomfortable feelings before we can get adjusted to it, and our comment in such cases might be 'Well, I never realized . . .'.

The reading of a book is not, of course, in all ways parallel to a physical event, and some people will speak contemptuously of 'book-learning' and call it mere 'second-hand' experience. This is only partly true; if we take note of the skill in communication of many authors, and the power of imagination in many readers, there is no doubt that experience gained from books can sometimes be even more powerful and valuable than the restricted circumstances of our own individual lives may permit. In addition, it is often presented to us by great authors who have a much sharper and clearer comprehension of it than we should ourselves have. The best illustration of this is that many people can look back and remember certain books (not necessarily 'literary' ones) which have seemed entirely to change their lives and open quite new horizons.

What is the application of such thoughts to the teaching of literature in schools and colleges? It is this; each work of literature that we introduce to our students should be regarded as a potential 'new experience', something that is likely to have a distinct effect on them. Each piece of literature selected should be capable of making a meaningful impact upon its readers; unlike Byron's poem in Mphahlele's schooldays, it should have a meaning which the student should be able to grasp, to understand, and (as the final proof that he *has* understood) explain. A work of literature may sometimes seem, to begin with, something of a mystery; but it should certainly not end as one.

Experience is essentially something that we acquire, rather than something we are taught. Unless we can see for ourselves the point of a piece of literature, it remains external, inert, relatively meaningless. The task of the teacher is not just to fill a number of empty vessels with miscellaneous information: his role is rather more like that of a midwife, whose job it is to help a new idea, a new conception into existence. In some developing countries, there are strong traditions of the didactic teacher (who gives forth information) and the passive-receptive student (who collects up information). Here we are arguing for a much more subtle, more difficult, and much more useful kind of process. The teacher of literature is not in too much of a hurry to tell his students what each piece of literature is about, dictate notes, synopses, character-studies and so on. His aim is to enable his students to discover *for themselves* what it is about, restricting himself to the making of suggestions and giving help and encouragement where needed. It is of little value for a student to be able to utter a statement to the effect that '*Macbeth* is a great tragic masterpiece'; he must be able to show *how* it is a great masterpiece, and he can only do this effectively if he can show *what it has meant to him personally*; and he can only do that honestly if he has gone through the process of detailed discovery, and genuinely 'experienced' it himself.

An experience is not necessarily a single, instantaneous occurrence (such as perhaps tasting a new food, or a new drink); it is not always something that can easily be summed up in a few words. The experience of a work of literature may be something that grows, and unfolds, and develops as the reader makes his way through it. *Macbeth*, for example, cannot well be summed up in a catch-phrase such as 'Honesty is the Best Policy'; the essence of the play is the complex and subtle development which it illustrates in the mind of Macbeth as he passes through moods of ambition, temptation, violence, remorse, revenge and desperation. It is often very helpful in the reading of literature to base the experience of it on the idea of *beginning* (what is the initial situation?), *middle* (how does it develop?), and *end* (how does it conclude?).

We have suggested that the teacher of literature must know how to be wisely passive. This does not mean that he is inactive or disengaged. On the contrary, his powers of imagination and insight, both into the literature and into his students' minds, will be fully awake, for he has many decisions to make. He has to decide how far he can expect his students to make their way effectively by themselves. He has to decide where and when it is necessary for him to give judicious assistance: sometimes he will need to provide items of background information which are necessary if certain points are to be grasped; sometimes a form of visual aid or practical demonstration may be helpful; at other times he may need to call attention to certain features or details of the language from which the work of literature is built up. Above all, he will be ready at the right moment (which is when students are reaching out or searching for an explanation) to draw from his own greater experience of life and of reading to give such explanations as will help them to see the significance of what puzzles them, in a clearer light and a more comprehensive relationship.

Literature as language

The study of literature is fundamentally a study of language in operation. The study of literature must always be based on the realization that each work is essentially the collection of words that are permanently available for the student to inspect, to investigate, to analyse, to build together, and no other kinds of external information, whether 'what the Introduction says', 'what the teacher says', 'how the teacher reads', 'what the pictures show', or 'what the critics say' can have prior claim on his attention. The experiencing of a work of literature, no matter how big or small, can only begin, and continue, with the reading and the study of a verbal text. Nowadays many of us do so much reading that we are inclined to take it for granted, but the process of reading is a highly intricate business – as we rapidly realize by puzzling over a page of characters representing a language we do not understand. However, as with other activities in which we acquire skill after much practice, we eventually learn to carry it out effectively (as we think) with considerable speed. Nevertheless there are often occasions when the symbols of language require more careful interpretation than the inexperienced reader may himself realize, and the most successful teacher of literature will be one who, apart from his insight into his students' minds and interests, is fully conversant with all the ways in which language works, and can see exactly how it works in any particular case. His knowledge of language will include such concepts as that:

(1) all language begins with sounds, which act as symbols for various things or ideas, and become words.

(2) 'words' can vary very much; in fairly limited ways in their forms (e.g. boy, boys, boyish, etc.); in very much more unpredictable ways in the meanings (e.g. *floor*, V; *floor*, N).

(3) words are grouped together according to certain patterns, into phrases, clauses, and sentences.

(4) various significant relationships are established between the parts of phrases, clauses and sentences.

(5) sentences (of one kind and another) are organized into larger systems, such as paragraphs, descriptions, stories, sequences of thought, and so on.

The teacher of literature (equally with the teacher of language) will be aware how language can be used for different purposes, to give information, to express feeling, to persuade, to organize, to conduct thinking – (as well as sometimes to confuse it!). He will be able to distinguish between language used to refer to *actual* things, situations or relationships and language which is used to create imaginary or *hypothetical* ones. He will be familiar with the sub-languages of dialect and register that are available for specific purposes within the totality of the language he is working in. He will be ready to recognize the different methods by which a language operates, whether by statement, by elaboration, by rhythmic effect, by comparison, by allusion, or by indirect means such as understatement and irony; and he will be aware of the special effects that can be gained by changing from one method to another whether explicitly or unexpectedly. Most important of all, perhaps, he will be aware that words actually used do not always represent the whole of the ideas that are being brought into consideration: the analogy of the iceberg is very useful here to compare the small part which is visible with the great quantity which is unseen.

Although he needs to have something approaching this comprehensive understanding of language, the teacher of literature will not, of course, always be itching to show it off. He will keep it ready; he will work *from* it, and be able, as occasion may arise, to produce the kind of explanation which will be useful, in relation to the work of literature as a whole, perhaps in resolving a difficulty, in clarifying an obscurity, in pointing out an interesting effect. In short, he will be standing by watchfully to see that his students are able to trace out and build up *all* the verbal signals that constitute the experience that each work of literature embodies. He will not be content with his students gaining just vague impressions, as was Mphahlele's teacher, but will guide their interpretation to ensure that they grasp the experience completely, both in its entirety and in all its details.

Now it is necessary to discuss the question of speed of study. Up to this point we have been analysing the psychological and linguistic processes which are involved in the reading of literature, and have seen that in themselves they are quite complex. It is of little use to attempt to compel any student to work faster than the rate at which he can comfortably take in what he reads. On the other hand it is very important that the practical study of literature must never be allowed to seem slow, or laborious (or 'dreary', as Whitehead put it in the passage quoted on p. 14): in fact, work on literature should be accompanied by as great a degree of interest and delight (the best accompaniments of learning) as can possibly be commanded. This means that the teacher must develop a certain *discretion* in relation to the literature he presents, to decide to what extent it can safely be left to speak for itself, or how much detailed attention it needs. Some literature is obviously of a clear open nature, with few complexities or difficulties and can be adequately experienced by quite rapid reading at the students' own pace, with just a little discussion afterwards of general impressions and perhaps of facts of special significance. Other works of literature of a more intricate nature both require and repay systematic interpretation, and may only give up their full meaning and beauty after something of a tussle. These two types correspond to the well-known division of:

Extensive Reading,
and Intensive Reading,

and in any well-planned literature course materials should be provided for both of these. Extensive reading of considerable quantities of written matter (such as stories, novels, etc.) provides practice at sustained, rapid, self-directed activity, particularly suitable for carrying out as homework. The final reward of good teaching and good organization in this sphere is to find students launching out into entirely voluntary extensive reading, as a personal pastime or hobby, without the need for any kind of request or compulsion from their teacher. (Here well selected and supplied libraries play their most important role.) Intensive reading (of poems, prose passages, etc.), where more detailed observation and concentration is required, is in a sense the basis of *all* reading, and is more obviously suitable for class work, when close contact between teacher and student, working together, fosters the real discipline of literary studies.

These two kinds of reading are complementary, and each, of course, can give its own particular type of pleasure and satisfaction.

Literary criticism

Some traditions of literary studies which teachers may have had contact with lay great emphasis on literary criticism, or literary appreciation as it is sometimes called (and the present author has himself recently published a book on the subject), and they may feel a strong urge, as they have themselves been trained at colleges or universities, to expect the same kind of activity of their students in secondary schools. Thus they may feel eager to rush into questions of 'evaluation', 'judgement', 'good and bad', 'approval and disapproval', and so on. Here we shall only say that this issue is complex and in some respects controversial, and sum up the situation in the following four points:

(1) The over-riding aim of literary studies must be the complete interpretation and assimilation of the 'experience', as embodied in the 'language', of works of literature. It is quite impossible even to begin discussion of merit until the experience has been completely comprehended.
(2) Value judgements often involve very intimate elements of a particular culture, and depend a great deal on the ability to make a great number of comparisons within it. Thus it may be very difficult, perhaps impossible, for second-language learners to see things as they would be seen by native speakers.
(3) If students feel that they are being expected to provide judgements which they lack confidence to make with any conviction, this will only inhibit their approach to the whole field of study and often distort their interpretation of elements which should be within their competence. Therefore literary criticism should be undertaken, even by teachers who feel proficient at it themselves, with considerable care, and certainly only at an advanced stage. In secondary schools in Britain, very few teachers consider it practicable to attempt much literary criticism before the Sixth Form course – even with native speakers.
(4) Proficiency in literary criticism constitutes perhaps one of the 'final achievements' of literary study, but a great deal of valuable experience can be gained by students whose efforts are made principally in the field of thoughtful, systematic interpretation.

A basic procedure

Although there are various forms of literature, we have seen that important aspects are common to all forms. We can therefore suppose that a standard method of procedure could be adopted by any teacher of literature, and a suggested method is put forward in the following pages. At the same time, we should emphasize that although there are certain fundamental stages which the study of a work of literature passes through, it is essential that no lesson should seem to fall into a set mechanical routine. The teacher will be helped because literature in its subject-matter and its expression is extremely varied; in addition to that, however, he must introduce variation into his lessons so that students are always kept alert, and ready to respond to many different kinds of stimulus.

The suggested procedure for a teacher to observe consists of the following stages:

(1) **Preliminary assessment**
(2) **Practical decisions**
(3) **Introduction of the work**
(4) **Presentation of the work**
(5) **Discussion**
(6) **Reinforcement (testing).**

5

The Study of Poetry

We deal first with the study of poetry because this raises in a concise way some of the most typical problems in the teaching of literature. Poetry has been accorded a place of honour in every culture which has a literature to boast of; poets have been hailed as 'prophets', 'makers', 'unacknowledged legislators'; and men of affairs (Sir Philip Sidney, Field-Marshal Wavell, Dag Hammarskjöld, Leopold Senghor), have been keenly interested in this form of expression. Yet the teaching of poetry in developing countries presents special difficulties, and many teachers are inclined to avoid it as long as they can. We must briefly consider the reasons for this, though the problems are found not only in these countries but even in those where students are being educated in their mother tongue. When teachers know how to set about this part of their work, there are *no* students who cannot be helped to understand and enjoy at least some poems.

There seem to be two kinds of obstacle to the enjoyment of poetry. The first is the thought that it is 'useless'. The world we live in is very practical and depends a great deal on commerce, on science (physics, chemistry, biology) and on technology (medicine, engineering). This has been notably expressed by Jean-Paul Sartre in *Black Orpheus*, whose explanation is of course somewhat political:

> It is the present circumstances of the class struggle which turn the worker from poetical expression. Oppressed by technical forces, he wishes to be a technician; because he knows that these technical forces will be the instrument of his liberation. If he must some day be able to control and direct vast enterprises, he knows that it will come about only through an economic and technical knowledge.

Most intelligent boys and girls understandably wish to acquire some expertise in those fields in contrast to which poetry seems only a matter of words. Nobody can land a million-dollar contract, launch a lunar rocket, or carry out a heart-transplant merely by 'talk', and so on. . . . It should not take a convinced teacher long to counteract such prejudice both by reasoned arguments (of the kind found in Chapters 2–4 of this book) and by instances to prove the contrary.

The second kind of obstacle consists not so much of prejudice as of memories of 'unfortunate experience'.

It is possible that with the best will in the world students have done their best to make sense of famous poems by famous writers only to find themselves baffled by such language as:

Calme was the day, and through the trembling ayre,
Sweete breathing *Zephyrus* did softly play
A gentle spirit, that lightly did delay
Hot *Titan's* beames, which then did glyster fayre. . . .

(Edmund Spenser)

If ought of Oaten stop, or Pastoral Song,
May hope, chaste Eve, to soothe thy modest Ear. . . .

(William Collins)

Breaking earth upon
A spring-haired elbow, lone
A palm beyond head-grains, spikes
A guard of prim fronds, piercing
High hairs of the wind

(Wole Soyinka)

Archaic spelling, familiar words used in unexpected contexts, obscure references, unfamiliar comparisons, nonsensical statements, chaotic sentences are just a few of the features which are liable to make co-operation difficult. All the more so, if the student is being told that he ought to 'enjoy' this form of literature and that it is 'good' for him. Also the field of poetry seems to be extraordinarily complex, for there are lyrical poems, epic, narrative and satirical poems; and before long the discussion is liable to bring in yet further technical expressions – metaphysical poetry, impressionistic poetry, symbolism, imagery, hyperbole, metre, and perhaps many other things besides.

How is the teacher of literature to steer his students safely through all these difficulties? We have already emphasized the importance of the principle of *selection* and with no branch of literature is this more important than with poetry. Even if we consider only the poetry written in the English Language (though the same applies to others), we quickly come to realize that the greater part of it was certainly not written for posterity, for use in school, let alone for students who use English as a second language. Often it was written not for straightforward communication between the poet and the man-in-the-street, but for highly sophisticated readers of one kind and another. Poets have sometimes thought of themselves, for example, as men of wit, and their aim has been to express themselves in as clever, amusing or 'puzzling' ways as possible. In many non-European cultures we should also remember that poets have been traditionally regarded as prophets and oracles, who deliver important truths, though often in indirect or puzzling forms. During the present century too there has been a considerable cult of 'obscurity'. Poets have not always concerned themselves with the familiar ideas of ordinary people, for many have attempted to extend the boundaries of human consciousness, teaching people to see things in a new way, and this does not always make for easy comprehension, though of course the difficulties may well be worth very careful consideration.

In spite of all these sources of difficulty, we can find a considerable body of poetry which will be both comprehensible and meaningful for students at all levels. There is no shortage of testimony; for example, the West African writer William Conton in the novel *The African* describes how his hero undertakes a kind of pilgrimage to the English Lake District which inspired many of the poet Wordsworth's works, and Ezekiel Mphahlele tells us in his autobiography, *Down Second Avenue*, how G. M. Hopkins

... kept me company in my lonely moments and when I climbed the mountains nearby to view the majesty, the grandeur that is Mushoeshoe's country.

When we have selected those poems which meet our criteria of selection, we shall realize that we have something which in certain ways has a very special value. Poetry is language which has been chosen and organized with great care and skill: in some ways it represents language at its most perfect, its most meaningful. When the language of a poem and its subject matter are in harmony, the student will find himself dealing with notable and memorable instances of the language he is studying in actual use. These remain in the memory, and may be valuable in themselves, and even more in the influence they may exercise upon the student's powers of self-expression. A further incidental advantage of poetry is that, as it is usually composed with close reference to the spoken forms of the language, it can be very helpful in the development of effective speech.

The teacher should make his own decisions in relation to his students' capacities, and remember that there is no special magic attached to 'big names' or established reputations. Quite possibly some of the 'big names' will provide some of the poetry which is suitable for study: on the other hand they may not. Some suitable selections of poetry have now been published (some are listed in Appendix A), but enterprising teachers will always be adding to their own collection new poems which they have discovered to be successful.

Perhaps the most important thing of all in teaching poetry is to preserve a normal atmosphere in the classroom. Neither teacher nor students should feel at the beginning of a lesson that they are on the verge of an experience which is either particularly 'holy' or particularly 'dreadful'. The kind of poetry we want to use is made of language just like anything else we read; and it conforms to the same principles, building up its 'message' with the help of individual words (and their various meanings) and syntax or grammar (with its various resources for extending, organizing, and qualifying meaning). Although poetry may sometimes be set out on the page in strange patterns, the basic laws of language still apply, and if it is necessary to jump from the end of one line to the beginning of the next to pick up the meaning, e.g.

> When I consider how my light is spent,⌐
>
>   ⌐ Ere half my days, in this dark world and wide. . . .

this is no more than we do when reading any written or printed matter. As for all the technical matters, such as metaphor, hyperbole and so on, we should certainly not be deterred by the thought of these. They make their contribution to the poem, without need for us to recognize and name them. When Shakespeare, for example, makes Macbeth say, at the moment of his final despair

> Life's but a walking shadow, a poor player
> That struts and frets his hour upon the stage,
> And then is heard no more.

any reader can appreciate the meaning and the effect of this, without needing to count up how many metaphors it contains. Certainly some poems will lead us into experiences of depth and complexity, and we may sometimes find our emotions strongly affected, but this will not always be so, for as the compiler of one very famous anthology has said: 'We shall do poetry a great disservice if we confine it only to the major experiences of life.'

Now we can go on to consider problems of classroom work in more detail, first in general outline according to the procedure suggested in Chapter 4, and then considering some particular poems as examples.

1 Preliminary assessment

The teacher's preliminary study of the poem will enable him to gain a good grasp of it before introducing it to his students; to check any facts which may need special explanation; to decide which aspects should be given special attention, and so on.

One of the most important things is to discover the 'approach' of the poem i.e. whether the poet is addressing another particular person, or mankind in general; whether the poem represents a conversation, or an internal monologue – whether its meaning is entirely on the surface, or whether there is an underlying meaning.

2 Practical decisions

Many poems are short enough to be read and studied in the classroom, and can usually be presented without any break. Probably too much preliminary information is a distraction, but the teacher must distinguish what is indispensable to the understanding of the poem from what can be worked out with the class in discussion. The teacher also needs to decide at what stage of study students should *see* the poem in printed form.

3 Introduction

This is a very individual matter, depending on the teacher's own knowledge and the features of each poem, and may be influenced by what the class has recently been doing. The problem can be studied from the demonstrations later in the chapter.

4 Presentation

Students will usually first become acquainted with each poem by hearing the teacher reading the poem to the class himself. Poetry is predominantly an oral art form: its true effect comes from being read or recited aloud by an individual to a group. Only in this way can its dramatic and rhythmic qualities be satisfactorily demonstrated and appreciated.

What use can be made of recordings of poetry spoken by famous actors of professional readers? Unless a poem requires the use of special dialects or other effects (possibly background noises?) beyond the resources of the teacher, the best use of a recording is to help the teacher prepare his own reading. From a professional recording he can, if he needs them, get suggestions on matters of pronunciation, tone of voice, emphasis, pausing and so on, though he should remember that he himself is a 'professional', and that other people's interpretations are not necessarily any more authoritative than his own. At a later stage of study the class could hear the recorded version for additional interest. The teacher might even record his own reading of a poem and use that in the classroom; as his voice is (presumably) well known to his students, the effect of personal presentation is fairly well preserved, and the teacher may have more opportunity of observing the reactions of the class.

If a poem presents material which will not easily be grasped at a single hearing, the teacher may well read it over a second time without comment or discussion so that its various elements fall into place in the listeners' minds. Another occasion for an immediate repeat reading may be when a poem has given obvious enjoyment.

5 Discussion

The sequence to be followed depends very much on the teacher's imagination, the particular poem, and the responsiveness of the class. In general the sequence of question and answer will follow the pattern:

General (first impressions)→Particular (detail)→General (conclusions)

Discussion will first of all be concerned with such matters as: Who is speaking in this poem? Who is being addressed? What is the situation? What has he just done? What is he thinking about? What does he want to do? Is he pleased/happy/frightened/anxious, etc.?

When it is clear that the class has understood the general idea of the poem, it will be time for some elucidation of the detail, but again making every effort to see that each item of detail is considered in relation to the whole poem. Among the things to be looked at will be the *syntax* (e.g. Will he definitely go, or just possibly? When? Under what circumstances? For what reasons?); more extensive aspects of organization (What kind of development do we see in the poem? When/how does the writer's mood/thought change? Where is the climax of the poem?); and probably the interpretation of *metaphor* (To what is he comparing A? How does it help to compare A with B?) and the clarification of any significant *allusions*. At this stage digressions can only too easily develop, and while a good teacher knows that a good digression is often worth following-up, sooner or later all the details must be referred back to the poem, so that it is again seen as a unity, though now a unity compounded of many details.

As all the details are gathered together, there will follow the final stage of generalization, but now of a rather more evaluative kind: Why did the poet choose to treat this subject? Do many people experience the same thing/ thoughts/feeling? How could this problem be illustrated in our own country/ from your own experience? What effect does the poem have on you? Does this remind you of any other poems, or stories?

One danger that the teacher should avoid is the possible temptation to exploit a poem for extraneous reasons, using it as a source of data for purposes other than the understanding of the poem itself. This is liable to happen especially if students are also concerned with problems of language-learning. It is tempting, for example, to point out that: Here is an example of such-and-such a type of conditional clause, or here is such-and-such a type of unusual sentence pattern. An investigation of the language in a way that contributes to the understanding of the poem is of course permissible.

6 Reinforcement

Not all poems may be suitable for further work, but if the poem has produced a favourable reaction the teacher may wish to establish it more permanently in the students' stock of 'experience' by means of either oral or practical activities.

(*a*) *Oral.* Students should as far as possible have the chance of reading a poem aloud in order to get the real 'feel' of it, but this should only be done after an opportunity for preparation (possibly for homework). How can this be managed? Not more than a few can possibly read to the whole class: one solution is to divide a class into small groups to read to each other. Whatever reading is attempted should be done well, showing intelligent grasp of the linguistic organization of the poem and due respect for any qualities of rhythm, drama or feeling it may have. If a tape recorder is available, students will always make a special effort, knowing that their voices are going to be recorded. (Of course every teacher of Literature should have the use of a tape recorder.)

What should we think of requiring students to learn a poem for recitation from memory? Anybody who has forgotten what atrocities this can lead to should read E. M. Forster's short story *The Celestial Omnibus*! If teacher and students are working well together, memorizing and recitation can be an excellent thing. But nothing is so soul-destroying, and destructive of all interest of a poem, and of all poetry, as the kind of occasion on which students in turn stand up and recite mechanically a number of lines which they have learned – or, worse still, which they have failed to learn, so that the class hears nothing but an assortment of stumbling, disjointed fragments. Much can be done by enthusiastic teachers to rescue reciting from becoming just a dreary routine. Each student should feel that the task is important, and one of the best ways of making him feel this is by linking it with the 'social' instinct, such as by competitions within the class, assessments by fellow students, or festivals of spoken poetry on a wider basis. Throughout, the teacher should create a general value-system which gives more credit to intelligent interpretation than to mechanical memorizing.

Some poems (especially narrative ballads) lend themselves excellently to *dramatized* reading, which will be organized at first by the teacher, and later by students in groups. A special variant of this is *choral* reading, in which groups, or even a whole class can be involved simultaneously. There is tremendous scope for practical work here, too much for the present book to describe in detail. Some poems are particularly appropriate for choral reading, especially those which present the point of view of a group, e.g. 'We are they who come faster than fate. . . .' (James Elroy Flecker *War Song of the Saracens*).

(*b*) *Practical.* Various kinds of written work can be associated with poetry. Even writing out a poem is of some use; this may come in as a test of memorizing or as an exercise in exact transcription. But such activities can be of much more significance if students are encouraged to build up their own personal 'books', or collections of poems and other pieces of writing they wish to treasure, embellished with the various arts of calligraphy, book-making, illustration, and so on. At times written work can take the form of providing an account or outline of a poem, if it has a suitable theme and structure. Other exercises can be more of an imaginative kind in which students are invited to write accounts, stories or descriptions suggested by particular characters, episodes, or even phrases from poems.

To illustrate how the above theories can be applied in practice, we consider in more detail how a teacher might set about assessment, preparing and conducting lessons with the following poems:

1. *Romance*   by W. J. TURNER.
2. *Piano and Drums*   by GABRIEL OKARA.
3. *On his Blindness*   by JOHN MILTON.

The method of exposition used in the following sections is an attempt, which it is hoped will be acceptable, to reflect the actual thoughts of an actual teacher. The approach and the interpretation are obviously personal to the present author, and are not claimed as the only ones possible. Chiefly they are intended to illustrate the *processes* of teaching.

EXAMPLE 1

ROMANCE

When I was but thirteen or so
I went into a golden land;
Chimborazo, Cotopaxi
Took me by the hand.

My father died, my brother too,
They passed like fleeting dreams;
I stood where Popocatapetl
In the sunlight gleams.

I dimly heard the Master's voice
And boys far off at play: 10
Chimborazo, Cotopaxi
Had stolen me away.

I walked in a great golden dream
To and fro from school –
Shining Popocatapetl
The dusty streets did rule.

I walked home with a gold dark boy
And never a word I'd say;
Chimborazo, Cotopaxi
Had taken my speech away: 20

I gazed entranced upon his face
Fairer than any flower –
O shining Popocatapetl
It was thy magic hour:

The houses, people, traffic seemed
Thin fading dreams by day;
Chimborazo, Cotopaxi,
They had stolen my soul away!

1 Preliminary assessment

(*Teacher thinks to himself.*) Hm! 'Romance'? What exactly does that mean
here? Something to do with Love? Yes, but what kind of love? – Seems to be
all about a young boy's 'day-dreams'. Seems to be drawn to a 'gold dark boy'!
What on earth are Chimborazo, Cotopaxi, Popocatapetl? Monsters? Bandits,
who stole the child and cut out his tongue? No, hardly. Mountains, perhaps?
– 'gleaming in the sunlight'. Somebody'll have to look those up on the atlas

(consults atlas). Whew! who on earth would want to go there? Doubt if *my* students would. Still perhaps they dream of other places – Lagos, Dakar, Morocco, Paris, London, New York?! – yes, the theme might be transferable. What exactly is that 'golden land', line 2? Not Ghana (Gold Coast), surely? – Now who was it who wrote a poem 'Much have I travelled in the realms of gold' – I wonder if that helps? Language? Yes, fairly simple: word order fairly straightforward too: a few slight archaisms, '*but* thirteen or so' (= only), 'to and fro', 'did rule' . . . Now who's 'the Master'? Why the capital letter? – the school master, I suppose. Seems to have a slow, dreamy rhythm. Probably what my old English master would have called a bit sentimental: still, boys are sometimes like this. Certainly worth a try-out. The speaker is 13 + : a good point of contact, perhaps even for younger boys than that.

2 Practical decisions

Straightforward reading O.K. Slow dreamy reading? Interesting to note the kinds of contrast in each section between lines 1 & 2, and 3 & 4: emphasizes the difference between the everyday world and the visionary world! Now how do we pronounce those names? I suppose the rhythm of the poem should give a hint. . . .

'Chim bo 'ra zo   'Cot o 'pax i

Yes, that seems right. Let's look up the encyclopaedia all the same. Quite a few things we can *do* with this poem: already I see drawings of Popocatapetl looming up in the background!

3 Introduction

(*As spoken to the class, with suitable expression.*)
Good morning, everybody. How're you feeling today? Not so bright? What's the matter? – School life a bit monotonous? Never mind, we'll soon be having exams, then it's the vacation. Anybody making any interesting journeys during the vacation? Yes, travel certainly costs money. Tell me, suppose somebody gave you a blank cheque, where would you like to go? Moscow! Cairo!! Johannesburg!!! Oxford!!!! Well, at least you've got plenty of ideas. Well, let's stop chatting, and get to work, shall we? Today, I want you just to listen to this. We'll find it in the book later. It's quite easy. There are a few puzzles in it, though. I'm not going to explain them yet – probably you'll be able to work them out yourselves. Here's the title (writes it up). You've seen that word before, haven't you? Yes, probably at the cinema. Still, don't jump to conclusions: most words, you know, have more than one meaning. Well here it is (reads)

'ROMANCE . . . etc.'

4 Presentation

In this case the class, having had their attention turned towards the kind of topic that the poem presents, listens as the teacher reads it. A first reading may be expected to give some idea of the theme, but cause some perplexity. A second reading aloud would follow the first, without any discussion, even if some students are already eager to ask questions or express opinions.

Finally, students might open their textbook and listen to the poem being read a third time, possibly by a good reader from the class, who has been urged to read it as closely as possible to the way the teacher had read it.

5 Discussion

This could be initiated by a series of questions such as the following:
1. Who is speaking in this poem? Is it a boy, or a girl?
2. Is he speaking aloud or to himself?
3. Is he in fact 'speaking', or just 'thinking'?
4. Is there a better word than 'thinking' to describe what he's doing?
5. Who, or what, are Cotopaxi, Chimborazo, Popocatapetl? People? – or what? What makes you think so?
6. What impression do you get from those names? Are they ugly names? – or what?
7. How did he react to the death of his father and brother?
8. Who is the 'Master'? What do you think the 'Master' would have to say about the boy?
9. What would you expect to see if you were looking at Popocatapetl?
10. What is the expanded form of 'I'd' (line 18)? What special meaning has it here?
11. What do you think of the attitude of the boy? Would you condemn it? Can it be justified? Why should he behave like that?
12. Why is the poem called 'Romance'?
13. What do psychologist's mean when they talk about 'living in a fantasy-world'?
14. Why do most people have special feelings of awe about mountains?

6 Reinforcement

This would be a reasonably good poem to learn, being simple, and melodious. It could be left fallow for a few weeks and offered as one of several poems to be prepared for recitation; but alternatives should be allowed – this poem might not be to everybody's taste. There is also obviously a lead out of this poem to further research into Chimborazo, Cotopaxi, Popocatapetl: their situation, description (see *Encyclopaedia Britannica*); possibly a brief consideration of the ethnography, history, and ways of life of the people in those countries. Research could lead to written reports (composition). Exercises in imaginative writing could include stories about the boy in the poem: scenes from his past life: what he would be doing 20 years later: conversations between him and his schoolfellows, etc.

There is the obvious possibility of students producing visual illustrations, perhaps embellishing the poem to include in their personal collections.

Other poems with a related theme which might be looked at include Keat's sonnet 'On First Looking into Chapman's Homer', or Philip Larkin's 'Poetry of Departures'.

EXAMPLE 2

PIANO AND DRUMS

When at break of day at a riverside
I hear jungle drums telegraphing
the mystic rhythm, urgent, raw
like bleeding flesh, speaking of
primal youth and the beginning,
I see the panther ready to pounce,
the leopard snarling about to leap
and the hunters crouch with spears poised;

And my blood ripples, turns torrent,
topples the year and at once I'm   10
in my mother's lap a suckling;
at once I'm walking simple
paths with no innovations,
rugged, fashioned with the naked
warmth of hurrying feet and groping hearts
in green leaves and wild flowers pulsing.

Then I hear a wailing piano
solo speaking of complex ways
in tear-furrowed concerto;
of far-away lands   20
and new horizons with
coaxing diminuendo, counterpoint,
crescendo. But lost in the labyrinth
of its complexities, it ends in the middle
of a phrase at a daggerpoint.

And I lost in the morning mist
of an age at a riverside keep
wandering in the mystic rhythm
of jungle drums and the concerto.

1 Preliminary assessment

(*After a private reading.*) Now this *is* interesting. Whole world's focused in this poem. African author, I see: in the fashion, managing without verse patterns, or rhymes, or even capital letters! A disciple of Dylan Thomas, it seems. Still, it makes consecutive sense. No 'blackouts' of meaning. Certainly an interesting way of presenting the dilemmas of a developing society. I wonder if there's too much foreign culture in this – concerto, diminuendo, crescendo, etc? At least a challenge, to see how far we can venture into those 'new horizons', as the poet puts it. I wonder which concerto? Duke Ellington? No, there's supposed to be a contrast. Perhaps Mozart. The poet seems to be musing over the anomalies of his situation in the modern world! Plenty of subtle words to emphasize the theme. Be best to try it with the Sixth Form; link it with their General Paper! Fifth Form would manage it well enough too.

2 Practical decisions

This poem obviously requires considerable background. Question: do we first lecture on Music, or do we introduce the poem and hope it will provide a pretext for some discussion on music and culture? Probably the latter? Possibly a bit of both. Idea!! – what about putting the whole thing including 'noises off' on tape. Perhaps the physics department would give me a bit of help. Let's see, we'd need . . . two gramophones, and a tape recorder, and I'd be the 'poet'. Good idea to use a bit of enterprise: perhaps students might work out something similar later on.

3 Introduction

Good morning. Well, how did you enjoy the Arts Festival Final Concert last week? What did you like best? The little drummer? Would you call the drum a musical instrument, by the way? What *is* music, then? How does African music compare with European? I suppose we need a few things which western 'culture' can bring us. . . . What about the contributions of African culture to the rest of the world? Jazz? Yes – what exactly is jazz, would you say? From what you know about it, would you say European music is similar, or different?

Anyway, I'm not altogether changing the subject, but I'd like you to listen to something that's been recorded on this tape.

4 Presentation

(*This is what might be heard.*) First comes the sound of drumming, fairly quiet, as might be heard from a remote village on the approach of an important festival. The drumming increases in sound, and then suddenly merges into a popular jazz, or 'highlife' number. This goes on for a time, then the sound fades away and remains as a subdued background as the first two sections of the poem are spoken with intense and rhythmic emphasis. At the end of section two, the jazz sounds return for a while. They fade out and the slow movement of Rachmaninoff's piano concerto, No. 1, is faded in, first the plaintive, sweeping, string melody, and then the interjections of the solo piano. This fades out and the voice takes up section three. After the words 'daggerpoint', the music builds up to a great climax, at which it suddenly ceases as if cut short. After a pause, the voice begins to speak the final section of the poem, slowly and poignantly ('I am *lost*'). As the poem ends, the sound of distant drumming is repeated, rising in volume, and both the jazz and the concerto are heard superimposed on it, a hideous din. This again rises to a nerve-racking climax, and then gradually fades away . . . to be followed by

Respectful silence

5 Discussion

Well, what did that prove? Don't let's bother about details yet. Yes, that African music and European music aren't all that different? On the other hand, they do differ in certain ways perhaps? What about jazz? Yes, very primitive, very elemental? Yes, like your heart beating, your pulse beating, your breathing? And the other? Intricate and complex, like the inside of a telephone exchange? Yes, that's quite a poetic comparison! But let's look at the poem itself. Then we'll play the tape again later. Here are some copies. Listen to the poem itself, without the background noises.

(Re-read poem)

Well now, do we suppose this poem is actually spoken, in an actual setting? or is it 'all in the mind'? Yes, it could be a civil servant with a house near the river, and a neighbour who plays his radio, or his gramophone very loud in the early morning. Yes, he might recently have had some quarrel with his boss, and the mixture of sounds seems to sum it all up!

What about those verbs in the first section 'hear'? – yes, that's a continous tense, *whenever I hear*. What about 'see'? When he says 'I see the panther, the leopard, the hunters . . .', does he actually see them, or is it in a kind of vision? Yes, his mind goes back to his childhood days? What kind of feeling does he try to give about the old ways? What effect does the jungle music have on him? What is the contrast between 'simple paths', and 'innovations'? What could he be referring to as 'innovations'? What kind of feeling is he suggesting in the words 'hungry feet and groping hearts'?

Now we come to the piano. Do you know that both drums and piano are classified as percussion instruments? What does that mean? But what would you say is the difference between them? What does the 'solo' effect of the piano seem to symbolize? What about those words *diminuendo, crescendo*, and *concerto* and *counter-point*? Are they English? Do you think they'd be, let's say, in the *Advanced Learner's Dictionary*? Did you notice by the way the *diminuendoes* and the *crescendoes* in my recording? Well, notice them next time. Anyway, here we have on the one hand the drums, on the other hand the piano: what does the poet think about his situation? Can you understand his feelings?

6 Reinforcement

Opportunities for research, and further 'cultural adventures', African and Western. Jazz, African art, famous collections and exponents. Definitions. Outline of European music: evolution from dance into symphonic forms. Even Jacques Loussier 'Play Bach' (if available).

Opportunities for students to write poems or stories of their own, interpreting the inter-cultural theme.

Debates: 'East is East, and West is West'; 'The dilemmas of the developing societies are also their opportunities', etc.

EXAMPLE 3

ON HIS BLINDNESS

When I consider how my light is spent,
Ere half my days, in this dark world and wide,
And that one talent which is death to hide,
Lodged with me useless, though my soul more bent
To serve therewith my Maker, and present   5
My true account, lest He returning chide;
'Doth God exact day-labour, light denied?'
I fondly ask. But Patience to prevent
That murmur, soon replies, 'God doth not need
Either man's works or his own gifts. Who best   10
Bear his mild yoke, they serve him best. His state
Is kingly: thousands at his bidding speed
And post o'er land and ocean without rest;
They also serve who only stand and wait.'

1 Preliminary assessment

Milton. Hm! one of the famous classics. Lived – when was it? – about 300 years ago – must check up on some of the facts of his life and time. Now, what's it really saying? Yes, I see ... first of all *complaining*, and then *accepting*. But that's a bit of a muddle in the middle – What about the language? – 'spent', for example (line 1). Here it seems to mean 'used up, exhausted': is that a meaning of the word we ought to know. Is it in *A.L.D.*?

Yes, meaning No. 2. So far so good. 'ere'? meaning 'before', of course. Yes, that's in *A.L.D.*, shown as 'old use, or poetical', still one's always liable to come across it. 'chide'? Yes, in *A.L.D.* What about 'exact', which seems to be a verb here? – Yes, in *A.L.D.* 'yoke'? Yes, in *A.L.D.*, picture as well. What about 'post', also as a verb? Yes, that's there too, meaning No. 2, 'travel by stages using relays of horses'. Well, the vocabulary doesn't seem too remote. Nothing to be taken for granted, but it's a good example of how words can vary in meaning. The main difficulty seems to be that involved sentence which goes on for how long, . . . for eight lines! Let's see, which is the principal clause? Must be at the end – 'I fondly ask'. *What* does the poet ask? Yes, whether God expects a normal day's work from someone who has lost his 'light', i.e. his sight. *When* does the poet ask it? Yes, 'when he considers how his light is spent, etc.' *Why* does he ask? – 'Lest He returning chide'. Ah yes. The Day of Judgement! Now there seems to be a problem with 'that' (line 3). Is it relative or demonstrative. Yes, I think the latter, modifying the object of 'consider'. See how 'consider' is followed by a double 'object':

> when I consider (1) how my light is spent etc. . . .
>   (2) that one talent (is) lodged with me useless which is
>   death to hide.

I see we have to supply an 'is', which has dropped out: also presumably later in the same line, 'though my soul (is) more bent To serve . . .'

Now why is the question he puts 'fond'? Which meaning of 'fond', anyway? – 'foolish', I suppose. Of course, because if he was a good Christian he wouldn't need to ask it: he would accept the will of God. Interesting, Milton presumably wrote the poem as a Christian, but there's nothing in it that a Muslim couldn't agree to. It gets a bit easier after the middle. 'Patience' presumably is a personification, probably 'second thoughts' within him. 'Who' (line 10) a pitfall! *Not* a question, but means 'whoever'. And what about 'state'? 'kingdom' or 'condition'? almost seems like the two together. Rather a good representation of God – not unlike one of the Obas or Emirs or traditional rulers.

Well, it's certainly an intricate piece of work. Can we get something out of it, without getting bogged down in sentence analysis? – or sonnet form (a b b a , a b b a , c d e , c d e,)? Certainly the subject is topical enough. And the theme of 'service' is also rather topical.

Now what about that 'talent' and 'day-labour'? – sounds familiar. Isn't it connected with a parable; yes! the 'parable of the talents'. Where is it? Yes, Gospel of St Matthew, Chapter 25 – one of those rather 'hard' parables. Still, didn't So-and-so at college call it the 'blue-print for all education'? – Why not ask the Principal to have it read at Morning Assembly before we actually look at the poem? . . .

2 Practical decisions

Not an easy poem, especially from the point of view of syntax. Could be given a quick reading just for the general impression. But it could be worth while to inspect its construction carefully. Also, we'll set the poem in the context of Milton's life and time: they're not so different from our own in some ways – Civil Wars, etc.!

3 Introduction

Good morning. Well, what do we think about the latest proposals for 'voluntary service'? What do you think about the idea of 'service' in general?

Is it any more than a relic of feudalism, slavery, and so on? Why is there, for example, a V.S.O. movement, and the Peace Corps? Neo-colonialism? Political infiltration? Hanging on to 'markets'?!! I wonder. Anyway, let's come back to that later. I wanted to ask what you thought about that reading in Assembly this morning. What *was* it? Yes, the 'parable of the talents'. Odd, isn't it, that talents meant 'money', while now it means something rather different. What was the parable telling us, anyway? Yes, that God expects people to make good use of their talents, of whatever kind! Would it still have any meaning, do you think, for anyone who didn't believe in God in the normal way? Yes, most people feel that if you have something, it's a pity not to *use* it.

This morning we have a poem – quite a short one; it's rather a tough one, though perhaps I'm exaggerating the difficulties. You've heard of Milton, John Milton, the English poet. When did he live? What is he chiefly remembered for? Anything besides literature? What was his great contribution to the cause of Liberty? Well, perhaps we shall learn a good deal more about that later on. Towards the end of his life he went blind. His later works were all composed in his head and dictated to his wife. The poem we're going to look at is called 'On his Blindness'. This is it. Listen to it first, and then we'll look at it in the book.

4 Presentation

The poem is read aloud, while the class listens. Special attention is given to the use of intonation and emphasis to indicate the sense-structure.

The first reading would probably be followed immediately by a second reading, which the class follows from the text.

5 Discussion

Many of the points of detail have already been commented on in the Preliminary Assessment. The general pattern of discussion would be as follows:
1. Who is speaking to whom here?
2. What does this internal debate discuss?
3. What does he most regret about his blindness?
4. What kind of idea of God does he seem to have, (*a*) on first thoughts, (*b*) on second thoughts?
5. What kind of consolation does he find?
6. What exactly does the final line mean?
7. You notice how the language in the early part is rather confused and clumsy, but becomes much easier towards the end. Can you suggest a reason for this? How does it match the idea of the poem?

6 Reinforcement

The immediate kind of reinforcement would be to prepare the poem for intelligent reading. This could entail a detailed study of the syntax of lines 1–8, for which some such framework as this might be useful:

Main Clause?	– I fondly ask.
What does he ask?	– 'Doth God exact day-labour?'
Why does he ask?	– Lest He returning chide
When does he ask?	– When I *consider*
What does he consider? –	(i) how his life is spent.
	(ii) that one talent . . . useless . . .
With what 'qualification'	
is it 'useless'?	– though his soul (is) bent to serve

Perhaps a paraphrase might be a useful means of getting close attention to the structure and the meaning. More extensive reinforcement might consist of research or further reading in the background of the poem: e.g.

1. What was happening in England at that time?
2. Interesting aspects of Milton's life and works.
3. Blindness. How would a person be affected by it? Does the poem give the effect of being written by a blind man? ('dark world and wide')
4. Religious doctrines. Ideas of God, the jealous God, the loving God, the God of Majesty, what is God?. . . .

6

Work with Prose Fiction

In this chapter we are concerned principally with the novel (and to a subsidiary extent with the short story); other forms of prose literature are dealt with in Chapter 8. Here the teacher in a developing country is likely to feel on safer ground, for prose fiction of many different types (and qualities!) is a well-recognized part of modern culture. The novel has the obvious advantage of being written for the general reader, and tends to employ fairly common varieties of the language. It also lends itself to individual, private reading, and this is particularly valuable, for the reading of stories in which the student can rapidly become absorbed and which will familiarize him with large *quantities* of language. A fair amount of work has also been done by educators and publishers in preparing editions and series of works, progressively graded for language learners at the early stages, though teachers must not remain dependent on these for too long, but 'wean' their students on to the reading of unabridged, original works as soon as possible.

From the more general educational point of view, it must also be recognized that, although some of the prose fiction in circulation is often of little value (some would even call it 'corrupting'), the novel is a literary form which has engaged the attention of a large number of the notable writers of the last two hundred years, and the body of prose fiction in the English language is capable of providing educational experience of unique value. Furthermore, if well selected and imaginatively taught, this form of literature can develop considerable enthusiasm and devotion in students, and easily leads on to extensive personal reading.

While one of the advantages of the novel is that it can be read privately at the natural speed of the individual reader, this may also cause some problems for the class teacher who will feel that he should not hold up the faster readers but must at the same time give help and encouragement to the slower readers, and also keep in reasonably close contact with all students' understanding and appreciation of what they are reading. Undoubtedly work on prose fiction is a field which demands a good deal of flexibility from the teacher, and some degree of individual or group work may be necessary. The principal aim should probably be to have some of both kinds of reading in progress (both intensive and extensive), so that nobody need be left inactive yet everybody will be moving forwards.

Underlying both kinds of work of course, there are certain basic principles, which are appropriate throughout, though with modification according to particular circumstances. First of all we shall consider in more detail some of the problems involved in the development of a general reading habit.

1 General reading

Teachers will know, from their own experience as students, that the desirability of extensive reading is easily enough stated as an ideal, but is by no means easy to promote, especially in developing countries where many factors (shortage of money, lack of privacy, short hours of daylight and uncertain supplies of artificial light[1]) make it difficult, and where also the whole cultural tradition is oral (based on the spoken word) rather than literary. In addition, at the present time in history, the whole world tends to move away from dependence on the printed word towards the aural visual culture of electronic machines (radio, telephone, gramophone, television) and the illustrated magazine, and there are influential prophets (for example, Marshal MacLuhan, the Canadian sociologist) who seem to argue that we should surrender to this tendency, and that the era of the printed word has been merely a passing phase in the history of mankind. Everyone would agree that the spoken word is supremely important, for all human contacts are basically personal, and many kinds of information and experience can best be conveyed by audio-visual means. Nevertheless the printed word will always possess considerable advantages, especially in education. For example, it allows the possibility of analysing and examining closely the detail of what is communicated, particularly the forms of language used; it also gives ample scope for selecting precisely what suits a reader's own personal interests so that the building up of knowledge and experience can proceed systematically. In a way, too, the process of reading, which involves both the senses and the mind, enables a reader to 'make his own' of what he reads; whereas information presented to the senses of sight and hearing remains relatively external. The reading habit should therefore not be allowed to die; and it is in schools and colleges that it is most easily fostered. Let us consider the problem in more detail, under the headings of *Example, Suggestion, Provision* and *Reinforcement*.

EXAMPLE. The most fundamental thing seems to be to impart the habit by a process of demonstration and example. This must be given in the first place by the teacher himself, who can best illustrate the value and the power of a wide background gained by reading. He must, of course, avoid the dangers of alienating his students by parading a pedantic knowledge of books. What he must aim to do is to show how the resources of his own reading can be made to illuminate the basic interests of his students, whether their personal problems, their social situation, or the world in general as they see it. A good teacher of literature can do much to stimulate a readiness to follow his

---

[1] The Emir of Kano in Nigeria once gave instructions that the street lighting in the city should not be turned off so early so that secondary school boys would have better facilities for doing their homework!

example by producing from time to time a new story, essay, or poem which surprises them by its *appropriateness* to what concerns them in their own particular situation. He will also judiciously make use of allies among his students: those who show most resourcefulness should have opportunities of presenting their discoveries to the class, and if spontaneous admiration is evoked in the class (rather than by praise from the teacher) so much the better. To encourage a readiness to contribute, it is a good idea to make occasions for every student in the class to produce something he has come across, of interest, allowing perhaps an average of 5 minutes each, or even less, and showing appreciation of everybody's efforts, no matter how modest to begin with.

SUGGESTION. The teacher must do more than give examples. In proportion as he manages to stimulate a willingness, he must also suggest how it can be followed up. Thus he must suggest what books, periodicals, etc. might be read, and also where they can be found. The most helpful thing he can do is to provide a reading list of authors, titles, and topics which are likely to have a genuine appeal to students at any particular level. To some extent, the provision of reading lists may be 'institutionalized', i.e. worked out by all the teachers with suitable experience in a particular school, town, or area. It is important that reading lists should be built up from teacher's actual experiences of students' reaction to books, and not just copied from catalogues. Reading lists of course, should be duplicated so that each student can have his own copy, and may perhaps tick off items as he goes along.

PROVISION. Reading lists should always be linked as closely as possible with what students can be expected to find without undue trouble or expense. In some places there may be public libraries, and teachers should make it their business to know what is available there, and indeed to make suggestions to the authorities of what they would like to see added. In other cases, the school or college itself will have to make almost all the provision; teachers and managers should ensure that funds, premises and personnel are available, according to local means, for the provision of libraries which are well cared for, well stocked, and convenient. Efforts must be made to encourage the use of libraries for general reading, not only for the writing of assignments. In some cases, teachers may be able to establish class libraries as well, so that the supply of books for general reading can be closely linked with the rest of the programme of study.

The books available must be of a kind that students can easily cope with on their own. Some more demanding works may be included, but the bulk must be capable of making a ready appeal and promote compulsive reading of the kind witnessed by the remark, 'I just couldn't put it down until I'd finished it.' An experienced teacher will know that there are of course certain kinds of compulsive reading matter (usually dealing with crime, violence and sex) which get circulated too easily; fortunately, however, there is no shortage of good reading material if teachers are alive to the problem, and it will not be beyond the skill of capable teachers to use what is good to drive out what is undesirable.

REINFORCEMENT. The enthusiastic teacher will find various ways not only of creating a reading habit, but of maintaining and extending it. Not making it seem too much of a labour (i.e. working by praise and encouragement rather than by blame and compulsion), he can get students to keep records of what they read, and even provide special exercise books, or loose-leaf folders for the purpose. This can be made into a practice which promotes a degree of personal pride in achievement. It can, of course, be linked with some famous precedents, for example, with the Elizabethan scholars' 'tablets' ('My tables! Meet it is I set it down', as Hamlet says), or with the practice of the noted scientist Charles Darwin, who tells us in his *Autobiography*, 1881:

> As in several of my books facts observed by others have been very extensively used, and as I have always had several quite distinct subjects in hand at the same time, I may mention that I keep from thirty to forty large portfolios, in cabinets with labelled shelves, into which I can at once put a detailed reference or memorandum. I have bought many books, and at their ends I make an index of all the facts that concern my work; or, if the book is not my own, write out a separate abstract, and of such abstracts I have a large drawer full . . .

Students' records could include information such as:
    title
    author
    publisher
    date of publication
    date read
    principal characters, or topics
    brief outline of story, or theme
    points of interest, or disapproval
    memorable quotations or extracts
    opinions expressed about the book by others, etc.

In some countries, specially printed record books using such headings as the above have been tried out with some success. Teachers, of course, have to be on their guard against treating such enterprise so as to induce fraudulent responses. In general, the best results will be achieved by the creation of a healthy interest in books for their own sake, not for marks, grades, housepoints, etc.

It may also be useful to increase interest in books by introducing students to some of the subsidiary aspects of 'bibliomania'; such as methods of printing, production, publishing, finance, copyright, typography, book-binding, special editions, microfilms, bibliographies, reference books and so on. Visits to a printing press, and to a really large library at a university or research establishment, would also produce good dividends. It is important to stress that books are not just objects of reverence, with vaguely magical powers, to be neatly ranged on shelves and never disturbed, but objects of *use* – as Bacon said, 'to be swallowed, . . . chewed and digested'. It is helpful if a teacher is ready to lend out copies of some of his own personal books, and even more to accept the loan of books discovered by his students. Much can be done in the way of informal contact and conversation outside the classroom ('Have you read any good books lately?'), while teachers may also consider various ways of 'socializing' the reading habit, for example, by encouraging literary societies and related activities, both inside the particular school or college, and on a wider basis. Various kinds of inter-school function may be organized, while possibly it might be worth while to get a famous writer (if he is a good speaker!) to come and talk to say Sixth-formers in a particular locality.

2 The study of a novel

Novels tend to have fairly complex structures, in which some or other of the following elements can be recognized and are suitable for discussion:

> Setting
> Characters
> Narrative
> Narrative technique
> Language
> Themes

SETTING. This means the geographical, historical, social, sometimes political environment or background in which the story is set. Sometimes it will be sketched out or described quite explicitly by the author before he begins his story (as is well illustrated in D. H. Lawrence's *The Rainbow*); more often, it will be disclosed gradually while the story is already in progress (for example, in Aldous Huxley's *Brave New World*) and the reader will need to build up the background as he goes along – which, of course, by no means reduces the interest. The setting of a novel may be unchanged throughout; in many works, however, there may be deliberate contrasts between two or more types of background (e.g. between life in the big city and life in the rural areas as in Cyprian Ekwensi's *Jagua Nana*).

CHARACTERS. A novel without these would be an impossibility, and one of the most consistent attractions of the Novel is that through the author's creative imagination we gain acquaintance with, and insight into, a great variety of human types and problems. It might be useful to distinguish two meanings of the word 'character'; firstly, to refer to an individual who takes part i.e. as *dramatis persona*; secondly, to indicate special notable qualities, or characteristics, of particular individuals. Thus it would be possible to say that some characters (first meaning) have no character (second meaning). A great deal of the interest in most novels, however, lies in the perception, assessment and understanding of the people we are introduced to. Sometimes the characters will be found to fall into categories of 'good' and 'bad', or 'sympathetic' and unsympathetic'; more often they will seem to possess various degrees of 'goodness' or 'badness', for most human beings have at least some redeeming features, just as no one is perfect. An important part of the reading of any novel is the attempt to determine the valuation which the author has placed upon each character, remembering that it will not be always an absolute clear-cut distinction between bad and good. Very often it is important to follow the author's explanation of what makes his characters *what they are*: many novels are, of course, notable studies in human psychology. Usually a student will have done what is necessary when he has grasped the attitude the author has intended to convey about each of his characters; occasionally it is possible to disagree with the author and say, for example, that the 'hero' seems a great bore, etc.

There are a number of different approaches to the presentation of character. So far we have mentioned the realistic type giving convincing pictures of possible people (e.g. Stephen Dedalus, in James Joyce's *Portrait of the Artist as a Young Man*). Sometimes characters will be found of a clearly exaggerated type, usually described as 'caricatures' (e.g. Mr Bounderby in Dickens' *Hard Times*) and these may produce special effects of humour, or satire. Other characters will be of interest because of their representative role, i.e. they present experience which is common to many individuals (e.g. Amusa Sango in Ekwensi's *People of the City*). Sometimes characters will seem to perform a more symbolic role, in standing for certain general ideas or themes (e.g. Captain Ahab in Melville's *Moby Dick* is in some ways a symbol of human idealism).

The interpretation of character in a novel can be a valuable exercise in the collection and interpretation of evidence, and students should learn to give consideration to the following kinds:

(1) what the author himself tells us (remembering the possibility of irony)
(2) what a character himself is made to say
(3) what other characters are made to say about each other
(4) what a character is represented as thinking, feeling, doing, or refraining from doing.

At times it may be useful to observe certain kinds of grouping or patterning amongst characters, or types of characters. Always, of course, the student will be bounded by what the author has put into the book and represented in the words used. Sometimes it is quite difficult to remember that characters have no independent existence outside the book; if he fails to remember this a student's interpretation can easily become distorted by his personal views.

NARRATIVE. Even in novels of great depth and complexity, the interest in *what happens and why* is of fundamental importance. Sometimes it is less easy to be sure of such things than might at first appear. The student will need to be ready to observe matters of personal intention and motive (both conscious and unconscious): but, of course, events can also be influenced by social machinery (e.g. the duties of a police-officer), by large-scale historical forces (various kinds of social revolution), or even by forces outside human control (e.g. a flood, or a plague).

The narrative element of a novel may be very simple, as in the autobiographical type (e.g. William Conton's *The African*), or it can be very intricate and full of surprises (e.g. G. K. Chesterton's *The Man Who Was Thursday*). It is also useful to bear in mind a distinction between external and internal actions. Students are sometimes known to complain that certain stories are very 'boring', because 'nothing seems to happen', and the teacher can help them to see that other things besides murder, robbery and sudden death are of importance in the course of human life. Even such things as the making of plans, the taking of a decision, the changing of one's mind, making a new acquaintance can be of absorbing interest.

Another type of narrative which is often of some interest is that combining certain aspects of fact with his fiction. Thus there are novels mainly concerned with various fictitious characters, but presenting them in actual historical situations (for example, Charles Dickens in *A Tale of Two Cities*).

NARRATIVE TECHNIQUE. If the narrative itself is concerned with What happens, we now come to consider *How we learn what happens*. Events normally follow each other in strict chronological sequence, and the straight-forward narrative, either in the first or the third person, proceeds steadily from A to Z. On the other hand, in real life our understanding of people and events is often built up only gradually, by piecing together different kinds of evidence, which do not always come in the most convenient order; some novels reflect this process in various ways. In fact, narrative techniques are obviously unlimited (we are reminded that one of the great educational values of the study of literature is that it trains us to be ready for anything). To mention just a few of the possibilities, we can think of the novel which is presented partly in the words of the author as 3rd person narrator, and partly in the 1st person narrative of one or more of the characters; the novel which is presented entirely in a series of letters exchanged between the characters; the novel which consists of a wide assortment of fragments of narrative, con-versation, newspaper cuttings, advertisements, and radio announcements (e.g. John Dos Passos' *U.S.A.*). One of the most difficult of all to follow is the kind which consists exclusively of dialogue; another is the novel which con-sists largely of internal monologue. One of the great masterpieces of fiction, from this point of view, is Conrad's *Lord Jim*, in which the whole life story and tragic death of 'Jim' is narrated by an old sea-captain Marlowe, who fits together in a series of evening talks what he has seen of Jim himself, what Jim has told him, and what he has learned over some years from quite a range of other observers.

Sometimes the technique of a novel will be seen to include not just a single narrative, but several, which are interwoven as the story proceeds for special effects of clarification or contrast (William Faulkner's *Light in August* is a good example of this).

LANGUAGE. There is usually a great deal to be gathered from a careful appreciation of the resources of language, the sub-families, dialects, registers, and personal 'idiolects' which may be employed in the course of a single novel. The most straightforward type of novel maintains a uniform style throughout, corresponding to the personality of the particular narrator or novelist. This method allows for many subtleties of description and definition. In other cases, however, authors will modify the language they employ, whether in direct speech or narrative, to reflect the thoughts and feelings of particular characters at particular moments. Again the range of opportunities is almost unlimited and a teacher is of great importance here in helping students to recognize the effect of such variations. As more and more sophisticated novels are chosen for study, language is likely to become increasingly subtle and indirect in its operations.

Let us consider, for example, a short passage from the novel *The Comedians* by Graham Greene, which in many ways would be a very possible choice for study at more advanced levels. The narrator, Brown, has recently returned to Port-au-Prince from New York where he failed to sell his hotel in Haiti, as the country had become increasingly isolated after the island .passed under the ruthless rule of 'Papa Doc' Duvalier. He is talking to the ambassador of a 'South American country', with whose wife he has been having an affair:

'How did you find New York?' the ambassador asked.
'Much ·as usual.'
'I would like to see New York. I know only the air-port.'
'Perhaps one day you'll be posted to Washington.'
It was an ill-considered compliment; there was little chance of such a posting if at his age – which I judged to be near fifty – he had. stuck so long in Port-au-Prince.
'Oh, no,' he said seriously, 'I can never go there. You see my wife is German.'
'I know that – but surely now . . .'
He said, as though it were a natural occurrence in our kind of world, 'Her father was hanged in the American zone. During the occupation.'
'I see.'
'Her mother brought her to South America. They had relations. She was only a child, of course.'
'But she knows?'
'Oh yes, she knows. There's no secret about it. She remembers him with tenderness, but the authorities had good reason. . . .'
I wondered whether the world would ever again sail with such serenity through space as it seemed to do a hundred years ago. Then the Victorians kept skeletons in cupboards – but who cares about a mere skeleton now? Haiti was not an exception in a sane world: it was a small slice of everyday life taken at random. Baron Samedi walked in all our graveyards. . . .[1]

To follow this conversation and the reflections upon it, to be really *inside* the minds of the two characters concerned we have to be ready to follow up some fairly slight clues and sense an undercurrent of meaning which is only barely hinted at in the actual words we are given. For example:

I would like to see New York: A considerable understatement. What seems on the surface a polite conversational remark masks a deep and desperate desire to get away from Haiti.

Perhaps one day you'll be posted to Washington: Here the author does make

[1] The passage is from page 130 of the Penguin edition.

explicit the clumsiness of the 'mild compliment', in relation to the supposed age of the ambassador (50), which we are expected to realize means he can no longer expect promotion to anywhere as important as Washington.

stuck so long in Port-au-Prince: The colloquial phase 'stuck' indicates the low valuation of Port-au-Prince and the length of time the ambassador had been there although unwillingly.

You see my wife is German: i.e. she belonged to the nation which had been at war with America during the Second World War.

but surely now . . .: Surely now, this implies, the war has been over for so long, Americans no longer harbour grudges against their ex-enemies.

as though it were a natural occurrence in our kind of world: Although the ambassador makes his next remark in a matter-of-fact way, he is aware that it is likely to be a shock to Brown.

the American zone: The American zone of 'occupation' in Germany after the Second World War.

I see: The speaker presumably has already begun to draw the conclusion that her father was a war criminal.

they had relations: An oblique reference to the way that many war criminals and profiteers (not only in Germany) had prepared retreats for themselves in other parts of the world.

the authorities had good reason . . .: This ironically informs us that her father was not just technically guilty as a member of a defeated nation, but was deeply implicated in Nazi crimes against humanity.

I wondered . . .: This nostalgic thinking back for a hundred years seems expressive of the shock which Brown has received and is trying to adjust himself to.

the Victorians: As regarded from the twentieth century, people who lived very secure and orderly lives.

skeletons in cupboards: Not literally, of course; a set phrase referring to Victorian ways of keeping concealed unpleasant facts about the past.

who cares about a mere skeleton now?: In the modern world, horrors are so common that we no longer even trouble to conceal them.

Baron Samedi walked in all our graveyards: Baron Samedi, as explained earlier in the novel, a character in the Haitian voodoo ceremony, associated with sinister evil, i.e. None of the supposedly civilized nations is really any better than the supposedly barbaric ones.

In addition to the allusions, innuendoes and understatements which all have to be interpreted, we can also recognize that, in spite of an outward politeness, the short, abrupt questions by Brown, and the short, rather painful, answers by the ambassador reflect the very difficult relationship between them.

Here then we have a brief illustration of how subtle language may become, especially when embedded in a complex and intricate context, and especially when it depends on incidents and information quite outside the immediate action of the story.

THEMES. As the study of a novel passes through all its phases, we often come to feel that the experience of the whole signifies something more than we have yet attempted to consider. Particular stories seem to be acting as demonstrations or commentaries on some of the universal problems confronting the human race; sometimes they even seem to be suggesting certain kinds of solution. So the culmination of the study of a novel will be to recognize and express, in terms which indicate that we have genuinely grasped them, the underlying themes which it may embody. Sometimes the themes may be obvious, as for example in Mark Twain's *Huckleberry Finn* (that racial discimination is contrary to genuine human feeling); or in Albert Camus' *The Plague* (that the privileged must recognize a commitment to the underprivileged); or in Chinua Achebe's *Things Fall Apart* (that there is an inevitable conflict between old and new in a changing society). Sometimes the themes may not always be so easy to identify; for example, there is perhaps some uncertainty in William Golding's *Lord of the Flies* whether 'civilization', as represented by the naval lieutenant at the end is a very precious, or a very trivial, attainment. To emphasize some remarks made earlier, we again stress that generalization about the themes of a novel must not just be given to students by the teacher; they must be allowed to *grow into consciousness*, as a result of their experience of 'living through' the novel assisted by careful discussion. Discussion must always proceed 'from the known to the unknown': 'There is no depth without the way to the depth,' and students must be seen to grasp relatively simple concepts, as of character, plot, cause and effect, before going on to more high-level abstractions.

3 Aids to the study of a novel

1. Choice of edition. Where choice between alternative editions is possible, see that students, or schools, or bookshops provide well-printed, easily legible editions, even if they cost a shilling or two more. A well-produced book suggests a pleasant experience to follow.

2. Getting off to a good start. In order to get his students interested in the book from the very beginning, the teacher may decide to read passages from the book before they have ever seen it. Sometimes an opening chapter or opening paragraph can be omitted (for example in Graham Greene's *The Comedians*) and the student can go immediately to a dramatic, or perhaps a humorous scene. Any visual aids which are regarded as necessary should be of good quality and ready for introduction at the right time.

3. Providing a structure of study. Short poems, as we have seen, can be dealt with on the spot. Until students are very experienced, the teacher should help them through larger works by stages. So, don't say, for example, 'Well, before we go, here's our next reader. I want you to read it completely by the beginning of next week.' It might be better to say, having read aloud the opening scene and discussed it a little – 'Well, that was the beginning of the next book we're all going to read. By next week, I want you to read the first two chapters. Then we'll discuss them to see what problems we find. Yes? Of course, if you want to, you can read on further, but it'll be better to get a good understanding of the opening chapters first.' In the course of his preliminary assessment, the teacher will have considered how the book can best be divided into sections: divisions may follow the author's chapter divisions, but it might be advisable to subdivide some very long chapters, or on the other hand group together others which form a convenient unit.

4. Making it real. The need for helping students to grasp a work of literature by making sure that they have an adequate and correct idea of any fundamental problems or concepts has already been emphasized. We now think, not so much of background items, as of how to bring the experience of reading the book vividly to life in the mind and feelings of the student.

A special possibility which we need to consider is the use of films which may be available of some of the more celebrated works of Literature – Shakespeare's *Henry V*, *Hamlet*, *Julius Caesar*, *Othello*, Jane Austen's *Pride and Prejudice*, Dickens' *Great Expectations*. The question is at what stage in studying these films can best be employed. It may seem that if a film can be seen at the very beginning of study, this will be best, for students will then have a correct idea of such things as costume, customs, social setting, as well as a very realistic representation of the characters clearly in their mind. On the other hand, many teachers would argue that the best time to see a film (or even a live dramatic representation) is at a much later stage in the period of study. For one thing, there is no guarantee that film versions accurately reflect the original book, and some of them, we know, depart considerably from the original, both in interpretation of character and handling of the narrative. For another, a great value of literary study is the demand it makes on the imagination and the inductive powers of the mind, and much of its pleasure arises from the reader building up and visualizing the people and scenes in his mind; it would be a pity to deprive him of this experience, even if his interpretation may be somewhat inaccurate in the first place. A work of literature, too, is something of tremendous intricacy, which we know takes many hours to absorb; a film, though nominally based on the same experience, is presented largely in two-dimensional images with a certain amount of supporting dialogue, and is usually a very much simplified substitute. We are not arguing *against* the use of film versions. Certainly, when teachers and students working together have arrived at a good understanding of a novel, it would be unrealistic to suppose that they should not see the film of the book. If, however, they see the film *after* getting to know the book, they will be able to watch it with more intelligent, and possibly discriminating, interest.

There are, of course, other ways of making books 'real', which may have a deeper effect, and involve students more intimately than the watching of films. We shall consider dramatization in the next chapter; apart from that, there are often opportunities for students to *reconstruct* scenes from the book in ways which enable them to grasp the essentials very clearly. Students can sometimes be asked literally to *construct* something based on the evidence available in the book. Many teachers will remember the enthusiasm with which younger students have made their own maps of Stevenson's *Treasure Island*. No doubt when students were studying Thor Heyerdahl's *Kon-Tiki*, many teachers encouraged students to construct a model raft out of local material, as a practical comprehension exercise, with close reference to the text. There are other ways of increasing the student's interest and insight:

1. John Bunyan's *Pilgrim's Progress*. Make an illustrated diagram of Christian's journey from the City of Destruction to the Heavenly City, using cuttings from newspapers and advertisements, etc. to illustrate the various episodes of his journey, e.g. Vanity Fair, the Slough of Despond, the Hill Difficulty, etc.

2. Edgar Allen Poe's *The Gold Bug*. Draw an exact diagram to show how they failed to discover the buried treasure at their first attempt, but succeeded at the second.

3. Joseph Conrad's *Nigger of the Narcissus*. Demonstrate by diagrams exactly how James Wait was rescued from the sick-bay after the ship had capsized.

4. Stanhope White's *Descent from the Hills*: construct a genealogical tree to show the relationship of the old Gidigil's descendants. It must always be remembered that such exercises are 'means' and not 'ends'; they are not opportunities for practical activity for its own sake but means of encouraging the detailed and accurate *realization* of the book in question. While teachers should watch for opportunities of employing such methods, however, careful reading, adequate testing and intelligent discussion must always be regarded as the basis of study.

5. Varying the method. Since the reading and study of a novel is often an extensive journey, the teacher can help a great deal by using different methods in dealing with various parts. The bulk of the reading will obviously be done by students individually and privately. The teacher may decide to read some parts aloud to the class, especially if there are effects of drama or humour which he can bring out. Some scenes may be suitable for dramatized reading, with narrator, members of the class taking different parts: almost certainly, of course, this needs some previous organization and students should have the chance to prepare their readings. To give every student a chance to participate, the class could be divided into groups, and a different scene allocated to each group.

It is perhaps hardly necessary at this late stage in time to advise against the class-reading method of dealing with a novel, in which a chapter is read round the class without preparation, each student in turn stumbling through a paragraph. Nothing could be more destructive of interest, more destructive of all the qualities of subtlety, beauty, or drama which a book may possess.

A good deal of variety can be introduced in the methods used by the teacher to test or assess the reading of various sections. Sometimes testing can be done orally and by general discussion; sometimes it may be done by the traditional ten short questions with brief written answers; sometimes, students can be invited to prepare questions to ask each other, possibly in teams, in the style of a quiz programme, with the teacher presiding as the adjudicator; certainly one of the best ways of activating a class will be to ask them to prepare questions to 'test' the teacher. Of course, when questions are devised by students, the teacher must be ready to supplement them, if questions indicate that they have not understood aspects of the book correctly, or if they have missed some important points. Probably 'reading for information' is one of the most useful methods: the teacher suggests in general terms, without divulging any precise detail, what the class should look for in the next section to be read.

6. Keeping stock. As a book is of some length and complexity, it is necessary for students to retain some impression of what has gone before, and it is usually helpful to compile a list of characters, with a few comments on each, e.g. if the book was *Moby Dick*, it would go something like this:

Ishmael, narrator, melancholy landsman who wants to go to sea.

Bildad ⎱
Peleg ⎰ Quakers, owners of the *Pequod*

Queequeg, Indian harpooneer, Ishmael's bed-fellow at the Spouter Inn.
Starbuck, first mate of the *Pequod*.

Similarly, it is useful to make a brief synopsis of each chapter. The kind of extended chapter headings used in some nineteenth-century novels can be used as a guide: e.g.

Chapter 10. Our hero makes an uncomfortable journey, but gains a new friend, hears something more about the object of his expedition, and prepares for his forthcoming ordeal.

Essential details would be recorded more explicitly than this.

7. Talking it over. It is in the process of discussion that students' own impressions of a book are confirmed, or if necessary, corrected. (While discussion is a characteristic part of literature study, this talking about real situations is also a fundamental element in language-learning.) Discussion, and the leading of discussion, is one of the subtle arts which a teacher of literature needs to develop to a high degree. There are two possible dangers in the way of fruitful discussion. One is for proceedings to be monopolized by one, or just a few individuals, whether the teacher himself or some loquacious individuals in the class, for this usually tends to discourage the majority. The other is for the exchange of ideas to be too random, pursuing one digression after another without any plan or objective. Discussion should be guided by two important principles; firstly to arrive at the truth, as far as possible (recognizing that in some issues finality is not possible), and secondly, to bring in as many individuals as possible. Discussion best arises out of questions, and a skilful teacher will devise sets of questions which pass from the factual, to the interpretative, and finally (if his students are mature enough) to the speculative. It is important for the teacher to know how to formulate the fundamental issue present in a book. In the later stages of study, he may experiment with the seminar method, and allot specific topics to individuals or groups for preparation prior to discussion by the whole class. Discussion of literature, of course, involves more than just talking, more than just having views; it should be a disciplined activity, and students should be encouraged to be sure of the grounds for their opinions and produce their reasons for them in public.

It is then but a small step to the writing of essays (of the kind expected in public examinations). These are in fact best considered as written discussions of books (or of selected aspects of them). Usually, especially in earlier stages, discussion in class should precede written work; but as students' confidence develops the process may sometimes be reversed. Students do not always regard the writing of essays with unmixed delight, but they should be encouraged to see them as convenient and important ways of working out their ideas.

In the course of discussion, it is of course possible and desirable to admit outsiders, in the shape of critics and commentators (and their books) who have also thought about the works which are being used in class. Of course, their opinions should be tested just like any other member's of the discussion group; and teachers will bear in mind that critical books are again a means to study, not an end in themselves.

4 Demonstration

Let us consider, as a practical example, how a teacher might plan out some parts of his work on the novel *Descent from the Hills* by Stanhope White, (John Murray, 1965), assuming that he is concerned with Class IV in a secondary school.

1. Preliminary assessment

Before reading. Written by a British ex-District Officer? Hm! Well I wonder . . . probably lots of reminiscences about big game hunting, jolly times at the Club, and so on! Probably no insight into Africans, or African affairs.

After reading. Well, quite different from what I expected. How nice to get a book one can read oneself with genuine interest! Remarkably objective.

Could have been written by one of the people themselves (Dougje, for example). Seems to have real insight into the ways of these hill people, their thoughts and feelings. Language? – simple, too; seems to have been selected to represent the rather simple outlook of the people – some rather fine speeches by some of the old men. Characters a bit confusing at first, but we can easily get them sorted out. Odd names! – Kumbandandia, etc.!! Plenty of opportunities for linking up with history, and geography (where exactly *are* those Mandara Hills?). And, of course, themes – a real gift here: problems we all know and can't escape from; but thank heavens for a change from *Things Fall Apart* and *The River Between* (no disrespect to Achebe or Ngugi)! Yes, I can definitely see a use for this book. Absorbing, and yet demanding. Surprised they've not got this on the School Cert. syllabus!

2. Decisions. Students will need some help in getting through this. Not too long though. Sixteen chapters, I see. No titles? That's one thing we can do. Don't suppose any of them will know that area (any more than I do). We'll certainly have to do some map-work; probably in the end a detailed sketch-map to illustrate the events of the story (Wakara, Wala, Pulke, Madagari, Kerawa, Kukawa, Maiduguri, etc. etc.). Yes, a list of characters will definitely be useful: a family tree, too, for the old man's descendants and their various wives. I wonder what the class is doing at present in history; perhaps it will link up! Arabs, Germans, Second World War, 'Chindits'? I see the author has published his memoirs (*Dan Bana*, Cassell, 1967): be interesting to see if there's much material for comparison there.

3. Introduction. Good morning, class! Well, what's in the news today? – Really? – Hm? – Oh dear! What a world we live in! What do you think you'll be doing in twenty years' time? – riding in a Cadillac, or working in a lunar salt mine? Tell me, who first used an expression about the 'wind of change'? What did he mean by it? Can you remember any other stories or poems we've read on this subject? – Yes? – Yes, very good! – Yes, of course! What about that one 'In Time of the Breaking of Nations'? Yes, you're quite right, in that one Hardy was more interested in the *un*changing aspects of human life ('Things will go onward the same Though dynasties pass'). Tell me, now, would you say change is a good thing, or a bad thing? – Yes, that's very true: it can be good in some ways, and bad in other ways. Well, we shall have plenty of opportunity to think about this, as we read our next novel, *Descent from the Hills*. Here it is. Anyone ever heard of this before? Who can tell me when it was first published? Good. Now, that's all I'm going to say at the moment. I want to see how much you can find out for yourselves. You can begin reading it now and finish Chapter 1 for homework; tomorrow we'll see how you've got on with it. If you think you need any books of reference, well, help yourselves! – ? Yes, you *can* read more than the first chapter if you want to, but give special attention to Chapter 1 because that's what we'll be talking about tomorrow. By the way, be sure to have your atlases with you tomorrow.

4. Presentation. *Chapter 1.* The teacher has decided to 'realize' the opening chapter by means of a series of short, informal questions. The lesson might be based on the following:

When does the story begin? What have you discovered about the setting? Who seems to be the principal character? What position does he occupy? What kind of community is it? Would you call it primitive, or what? What makes you think so? Would you say it was well organized? Tell me the names of some of the villages mentioned. What is the opening event of the story? Who was the child's mother? Where had she come from? What had led to the feud? Can you remember how Kumbandandia had captured her? Who was her first husband? What happened to him? Did you notice how Kumbandandia, in his marriage, was following a famous precedent? Why did Ahe not go back to her parents' village to give birth to the child? It says on page 20 that 'Ahe began to realize she was lucky': how was she lucky? Where was life safer, on the hills or on the plains? What made Kumbandandia's father suspicious of the new child? Why did he advise Kumbandandia to kill it? But, you remember, the child was born ten months after Kumbandandia had married her: how could he suspect it was not Kumbandandia's? How did (let's call him K for short) K decide the matter? What name was given to the child? Where did the name come from? What other things put Dougje's life in danger in his early years? What eventually saved him from being sacrificed? Who was the famous character in the Bible who nearly sacrificed his son? How had Ahe prepared the sign? Would you say she was cruel? What does the future seem to hold for Dougje?

Having rehearsed the detail of the chapter, there might be time to discuss some more general issues, such as:

(a) Does this chapter give a favourable picture of a primitive community?
(b) Can we rightly say that it was primitive? What features (if any) seem to make it so?
(c) Do children always inherit the physical characteristics of their parents? What have you learned in Science about the mechanisms of heredity?

Chapter 2. (The teacher perhaps decides on a different method to develop interest, already created and to speed up the reading.)

Good, now let's get on with the story. For next lesson, I want you to read Chapter 2. There are several important things I want you to look out for in this chapter, and you can tell me about them tomorrow. Here they are? (Questions either written up on the blackboard, or dictated.)

(1) Who becomes the next Gidigil of Wakara?
(2) What are the ceremonies and procedures connected with the appointment of a new Gidigil?
(3) What unfortunate events attended the new appointment?
(4) How do the evil omens seem to be fulfilled?
(5) What is Kumbandandia's act of personal heroism?
(6) How does Dougje get on as he grows up?

Next day these questions are revived, and the class may be expected to volunteer their answers with some enthusiasm. The teacher can elicit as much further detail as he feels there is time for. Perhaps he notes, in passing, that the debate of the clan leaders, partly verbatim but leaving much to the imagination, is something that could later be used for composition work, possibly even for dramatic treatment.

So, using the various methods available, the class will work its way through the book bringing it to life as they go.

5. Activities. During the course of their study, probably after the first reading, the following are some of the activities which might be undertaken:

(1) Diagrams showing the relationship of the various Wakara clans.

(2) Genealogical tree showing descendants of the old Gidigil, including such dates as are mentioned or can be inferred from the narrative.

(3) Detailed sketch-map of the area which the story covers, showing relative positions of the principal villages, distance to larger towns, points of the compass.

(4) Diagrams to illustrate some of the notable scenes; the capture of Ahe, the first motor-car, Pompomari.

(5) Subsidiary research into such topics as:
    Slavery
    Rabeh, the 'Arab' invader
    European colonization of the North Cameroons
    How the Second World War affected Africa. (Spitfires)
    The 'Chindits'
    Ethnography and Languages of the area.

(6) Debates centred on some of the principal crises of the novel, e.g.
    (*a*) The election at which Kumbandandia was appointed Gidigil.
    (*b*) Attitude towards innovations such as: firearms, tax, forced labour.
    (*c*) The attempt to open the black iron box.
    (*d*) The wish of the young men to sack Gwoza.
    (*e*) What leadership is suited to the clans after the young men have been away in the army?
    (*f*) The pros and cons of European Colonialism.

6. Discussion. Oral or written discussion might be based on topics, some more literary, some more sociological, such as:

(1) What kind of characterization is employed in this novel?

(2) 'The life story of Dougje symbolizes the pangs of a community in transition.' Discuss.

(3) 'Suit the word to the action' (*Hamlet*). Show how the language in this novel is modified to suit various occasions.

(4) Describe the traditional social structure of the clans, showing how this is related to their religion, mythology, and rituals.

(5) 'Individual and social themes are interwoven.' Show how the novel, while centred upon a few individual lives, also makes use of local

customs. (Childbirth, Marriage, Coming of Age, Blood-feuds, Superstition, etc.)

(6) What picture do you build up of the economic basis of life in these communities (*a*) in the traditional era (*b*) in the transitional phase? What would you propose as a basis for their security and welfare in the future?

(7) What evidence does this novel produce which bears on the question of the 'closed' and the 'open' society. (See article by BERNSTEIN, *New Society*, 14/9/67.)

(8) Possible exercises in imaginative reconstruction of the kind described in Chapter 9.

5 Short stories

Everything that has so far been said applies, with appropriate modification, to the selection, presentation and study of short stories. These may be found, of course, in special collections, but many appear from time to time in periodicals and a shrewd teacher will build up his own collection for use at various levels, doing his best to exclude the more trivial and worthless ones which sometimes appear in the course of periodical journalism. Since they are short, stories of this kind are usually somewhat restricted in their scope, number of characters, etc. On the other hand, they have the great practical advantage of being more manageable: a story can often be read to a class at a single sitting, or studied as a single assignment, whether in or out of class. The teacher has the advantage that the whole story can be experienced simultaneously by the whole of his class, which often makes discussion easier.

The short story, also, invites comparison and imitation, and is easily connected with the kinds of written assignments students themselves can be expected to do (this is considered at greater length in Chapter 9).

7

The Study of Drama

Drama is a literary form supported by the most ancient traditions, firmly embedded in the social customs of cultures throughout the world, and well known for the excitement and enthusiasm it produces both in performers and spectators. It is also a literary form which is capable of adaptation for students of all ages. Being closely linked with the fundamental instinct of imitation – which obviously implies a close degree of observation – its value in education is becoming widely appreciated. Educationists see Drama as a means whereby the young can progress towards maturity by trying out and experimenting with various roles which they need to have some appreciation of in order to obtain a full grasp of the world they are entering:

> Drama, the novel, history . . . built on the paradox of human choice, on the resolution of alternatives. They are in the best sense studies in the causes and consequences of choice. It is in their gripping quality, their nearness to life, that we can, I would urge, best make personal the dilemma of the culture, its aspirations, its conflicts, its terrors. . . . In some considerable measure we have intellectualized and made bland and good-natured the teaching of the particulars of history, of society, of myth. I would urge that in fashioning the instruction designed to give children a view of the different faces and conditions of man, we consider more seriously the use of this most powerful impulse to represent the human condition in drama and, thereby, the drama of the human condition.
>
> J. S. BRUNER, *Towards a Theory of Instruction.* (1967)

Nevertheless, while there may be a great readiness to enter into this field of literary study, it is not always easy for teachers to decide what material to use, what methods to employ, and how to deal with some of the set-backs they may encounter. The author has a vivid memory some years ago of some teachers of English in a large African university city being invited to take part in a reading of Robert Bolt's *A Man for All Seasons*, which was at that time a School Certificate setbook. Copies were distributed, characters and narrator appointed, and reading began; in spite of the fact that all were teachers of some experience, many of them graduates, the extremely dull, flat and unprofitable result was so uninspiring as to be, if not entertaining, at least very instructive. The present chapter therefore attempts to chart the field of Drama, warning where difficulties may occur, and pointing out how the possibilities it offers can be exploited to the best advantage.

It is essential to remember that Drama is not just the description or discussion of events from real life: it is the re-*creation* of real life ('the imitation of an action' – as Aristotle defined it centuries ago), and makes use of all the constituent elements of real activity. These obviously include language, but such things also as movement, position, gesture and facial expression. It should be noted, too, that the language we are concerned with is above all the *spoken language*. This means that we are able to make use of the varied and subtle expressive resources of language, such as intonation, pitch, volume, emphasis, hesitation and so on.

In preparing for any dramatic performance, or in studying any dramatic text, the principal aim is to consider how the action will both appear and sound under conditions of live performance. This will not be easy for students who have no personal acquaintance with the conditions of dramatic performance, and teachers intending to teach drama have a responsibility to ensure that their students gain this kind of familiarity. In some cases, the local environment may provide plenty of experience (cinema and television, of course, provide some substitute for genuine theatrical experience); in other cases, teachers may have to create and illustrate dramatic procedures much more from their own resources.

There might seem to be an essential difference between the study of a dramatic text and the preparation of a dramatic text for actual performance, but, as will be made clear, this is a difference which we should seek to minimize. In the first place, it is necessary to remember that Drama, throughout the world, falls into a number of different forms and styles, and it is usually important to understand what is being aimed at in each case, for the confusion of aims and effects can be disastrous. If, for example, the murder of Desdemona by Othello is greeted by prolonged laughter and cheering, or the witty epigrams of Oscar Wilde by stony silence, it is evident that something has gone wrong.

It would need an extensive course on Drama to define and illustrate all the different possibilities. The main lines of distinction are indicated by key terms such as Tragedy (involving sympathy with the unfortunate) and Comedy (involving laughter at foolishness). There are also the alternative possibilities of a life-like representation, or an exaggerated (burlesque) representation. The latter tends to produce the forms of Melodrama or Farce (both of which may seem wildly impossible, though often very entertaining). Again, we need to be prepared for plays which are seemingly realistic in every respect – in the language used, situations represented, costume, and effects required. In a different category are those plays which by contrast seem symbolic, in which the actions represented do not necessarily correspond with anything ever likely to be seen in reality. In these the language may be poetic or specially adapted to the symbolic nature of the play, mingled perhaps with music, dance, singing or ritual, and they are capable of being performed on a completely bare or 'unlocalized' stage, without any kind of scenery.

In addition, a student of drama needs to be aware that there is considerable variation in the dramatic conventions, or the methods of staging, which have been practised in different times and places. The principal possibilities are illustrated perhaps by the vast Greek arena, the mediaeval English street pageant, the intimate Elizabethan apron stage, the spectacular nineteenth-century proscenium theatre, and modern developments facilitated by radio, film and television. Styles of presentation again fall into two principal categories: either the type of objective representation in which the action is presented as a self-contained action, observed by the spectators as it were through a transparent 'Fourth Wall'; or the type which acknowledges the presence of the audience, by employing such devices as the Chorus (whether a group or an individual) which speaks directly to the spectators; soliloquy (a character alone on the stage speaking his thoughts aloud); asides (a character commenting to the audience on events and other characters on the stage); perhaps the placing of characters from the play in the auditorium and so on.

Not least, while teachers of Drama need to be aware of many things *other* than language in the study of a dramatic text they need to be more than usually aware of language itself also. The writing of a play is by no means a straightforward or an easy matter, as many enthusiasts have discovered to their cost. There is scope for a tremendous amount of skill in the selection of language, and in the interlinking of language with action. Nowhere in literature is the 'iceberg' effect of language more often encountered, in which the words spoken convey only a fraction of their total significance. Consider the following brief excerpt from Shakespeare's *Othello*, in which Othello asks his wife Desdemona to bring him a handkerchief:

Othello: Fetch it. Let me see it.
Desdemona: Why, so I can, sir, but I will not now. This is a trick to put me from my suit. Pray you, let Cassio be received again.
Othello: Fetch me the handkerchief: my mind misgives.
Desdemona: Come, come.
You'll never meet a more sufficient man.
Othello: The handkerchief!
Desdemona: I pray, talk me of Cassio.
Othello: The handkerchief!
Desdemona: A man that all his time
Has founded his good fortune on your love,
Shared dangers with you, –
Othello: The handkerchief!
Desdemona: In sooth, you are to blame!
Othello: Away!   (*Exit*)

Almost the whole of the previous parts of the play need to be recalled for the proper interpretation of these lines. We must know that Cassio has been dismissed from his position, and has requested Desdemona to use her influence to get him restored; that Othello has been incited by Iago to suspect infidelity between Cassio and his wife; that Othello fears this and yet sees the possibility of it because he is much older than her, and of a different race; that he has demanded some proof from Iago, and that Iago tells him untruthfully that he recently saw Cassio wipe his beard with the handkerchief which Othello gave Desdemona at the beginning of their courtship.

The most dramatic aspect of the passage is Othello's repetition three times of the simple phrase 'the handkerchief'. To a reader who does not bear in mind the whole situation developed in the play up to that point the repetition may seem quite weak. If however we can imagine the desperate anxiety which has been mounting up in Othello's mind, and renders him now almost speechless. we see that the simple unelaborated phrase, thus repeated with increasing anger and impatience is a perfect representation of his agonized state of mind.

Here too we must give due attention to the factors of spoken language. As Shakespeare selected those words for that particular moment, he was obviously 'hearing them' in his inner ear, and knew well what he could expect in the way of interpretation from the actors who would perform them. So students will sense the sharp contrast between the determined, rather petulant pleading of Desdemona, and the abrupt, ungracious demands of Othello. It seems fairly clear that Othello's words rise towards a climax of frenzy at the final repetition of 'The handkerchief!', after which he can no longer control himself, but has to rush away to conceal his agitation. How completely ineffective would be a reading of this scene which supposed that because the words 'The handkerchief!' appear three times in succession, they require an identical interpretation – which is, of course, all that the printed words can show.

That such problems apply not only to classical, or poetic drama (such as Shakespeare's), but to every form of drama can be seen by studying the following excerpt from *A Man for All Seasons*:

> *Cromwell:* I'm sorry to invite you here at such short notice, Sir Thomas; good of you to come. (*Draws back curtain from alcove, revealing Rich seated at table, with writing materials.*) Will you take a seat? I think you know Master Rich?
>
> *More:* Indeed yes, we're old friends. That's a nice gown you have, Richard.
>
> *Cromwell:* Master Rich will make a record of our conversation.
>
> *More:* Good of you to tell me, Master Secretary.
>
> *Cromwell* (*laughs appreciatively. Then*): Believe me, Sir Thomas – no, that's asking too much – but let me tell you all the same, you have no more sincere admirer than myself. (*Rich begins to scribble.*) Not yet, Rich, not yet. (*Invites More to join him in laughing at Rich.*)

Most of this seems outwardly an exchange of courtesies between two gentlemen in a friendly mood, containing nothing of deeper significance. However, when we read it with a full realization of its context in the play and remember that More, as Chancellor of England is in disgrace for refusing to recognize Henry VIII's attempt to make himself head of the Church; that Cromwell is the ruthless minister of the unprincipled King ('When the King wants something done, I do it'); that More has in fact been summoned in haste, with no regard for his convenience; that Rich, formerly a poor student and a protégé of More's, has grown wealthy by going over to the service of the Crown, even to the extent of betraying his master – this apparently innocuous collection of polite remarks reflects a sharp confrontation of opposing interests. A commentary on this excerpt might run on the following lines:

I'm sorry to invite you at short notice . . . good of you to come. Since More has had no alternative, Cromwell's words convey an insulting insincerity!

we're old friends: More appears to take a charitable line: formerly they *had been* friends. The fact that they are no longer (since Rich has prostituted himself to those in power) implies a gentle rebuke.

that's a nice gown you have: Earlier, Rich had been particularly sensitive about his poverty, reflected in his lack of good clothes. More had counselled him to guard his integrity, become a teacher, and not be so concerned about mere wealth. By noting that Rich now has a 'nice gown', More is quietly rubbing in the fact that Rich has allowed himself to be bought.

make a record: This signifies that More is to understand he is being officially interrogated, and has the chance of making a statement which would please the King, even if at the price of his own integrity.

Believe me: Cromwell slips into a fairly empty formula of colloquial speech. Then, pretending to recall that he is talking to a man of honour (also a lawyer), he realizes that his words may be taken at their face value. To counteract that, he brazenly admits that he is such an unscrupulous intriguer that no one can ever be sure of the truth of what he says. The effect is to mock at More's helpless position.

you have no more sincere admirer than myself. This ironical expression of admiration appears to be a flattering move, perhaps to win More's agreement to the King's demands.

Not yet, Rich, not yet. Here Cromwell is sneering at Rich's eagerness, which shows that he has no discretion in his recently acquired villainy. Cromwell, negotiating with More on the King's behalf, would not dare to be reported as an 'admirer'.

Passages requiring careful interpretation such as this do not of course occur only at isolated places in a play. As the action builds up, the interaction of word and situation becomes more and more intricate. In fact, when we interpret language as carefully as this, it becomes evident that even in what looks like a prose play, the language can become as highly charged with significance as ever in the subtlest poetry. No study which failed to discover these depths of meaning, no performance which did not manage to convey them, could be considered to do justice to the dramatist's intentions.

A further problem which may arise in the study of a dramatic text is to decide what kind of outward action and movements are to be thought of as accompanying the words which are spoken. Some dramatists are very explicit about this and describe everything in detail, e.g.

> (GUIL *takes a third coin, spins it, catches it in his right hand, turns it over on to his left wrist, lobs it in the air, catches it with his left hand, raises his left leg, throws the coin up under it, catches it and turns it over on to the top of his head where it sits.* ROS *comes, looks at it, puts it in his bag.*) – From the modern play, *Rosencrantz and Guildenstern are Dead*, by TOM STOPPARD.

But often the dramatist relies on his readers and producers to decide for themselves what is required. After the exit of the Ghost in *Hamlet*, Shakespeare gives no instructions as to what should be happening, yet the lines:

> O villain, villain, smiling damned villain!
> My tables, – meet it is I set it down,
> That one may smile, and smile, and be a villain!

seem to inform the alert reader that he must picture Hamlet searching feverishly for his 'commonplace' book, proceeding hurriedly to write something down. Similarly Macbeth's words, after he has enquired from the Witches 'whether Banquo's issue shall ever reign in this kingdom':

> Thou art too like the spirit of Banquo; down!
> Thy crown does sear my eyeballs: and thy hair,
> Thou other gold-bound brow is like the first:
> A third is like the former. Filthy hags!
> Why do you show me this? A fourth! Start, eyes!
> What! will the line stretch to the crack of doom?

give a very clear indication of what the audience expects to see on the stage, and also Macbeth's own reactions and movements at the same time. Problems of realization such as these may have to be encountered and solved over and over again in the course of a single play.

Now, we can begin to appreciate why the study of Drama comes in this book after the study of the novel. Drama is more complicated by several degrees! On p. 47 we outlined the things which are to be looked for, and discussed, in the study of a novel. In the study of a dramatic work, the same things (setting, characters, narrative, technique, language, theme) may still require our attention. But over and above these, we are concerned with the fundamental process of converting a printed text into a live performance, whether in the realm of our imagination as we read, or for an actual stage production.

How can the teacher of Drama best set about his work? As we have seen, the problems are very different from the study of a novel. Many teachers will be aware of the disappointing results which come from attempting the reading of a dramatic text with members of a class (it may be some comfort to know that even with native English speakers in secondary schools results are often not much better!). It seems essential therefore that, from the beginning of their acquaintance with a play, a class should receive as authentic an impression of the play as possible, and this seems to argue the need for expert assistance. It is possible that a teacher may be skilful enough and may have in his class a few others who can, with some careful rehearsal, bring out the essential dramatic qualities of the text in a classroom reading. A remoter possibility, with some kinds of play, is that he may be able to give a solo reading, taking a number of the principal parts himself. It would certainly be helpful for students to see a good stage performance of a play – but the word 'good' needs to be stressed, for a bad performance may only lead to a distorted idea of the real thing and promote disrespect instead of interest. At a later stage of study, students can be trained to perform the play themselves, or at least certain scenes of it – but this is no answer to the problem of initial acquaintance. The best solution is to make use of a good recorded performance, on disc or tape. A considerable number of notable plays are now available in commercial recordings, but it would not be beyond the scope of enthusiastic teachers to organize their own tape recording, with the help of colleagues and friends. The great advantage of a recording is that the performance can easily be controlled. While the dramatic development of the play should not be needlessly interrupted, the performance can be arrested at suitable intervals, so that teacher and students can discuss their impressions up to that point. If for any reason it is not possible to procure a good recording, a live play-reading can often be enjoyable and useful, and a resourceful group of teachers, making full use of local talent (e.g. amateur dramatic societies, or actors and actresses who are not normally concerned with education), can do a great deal to bring a play to life. In arranging a play-reading, whether it is to be recorded or not, the performers should add to the text all those elements of the spoken language on which the full dramatic impact of the play depends. If a certain amount of rehearsal can be managed before the play-reading, so much the better. At a later stage, when the full effect of the drama has been demonstrated and appreciated, class-reading would be worth attempting.

So far we have been discussing the study of Drama as though we are chiefly concerned with the great masterpieces of dramatic literature. Obviously this is putting the cart before the horse, and we must now consider types of dramatic work suitable at earlier stages. The local attitude towards drama may vary somewhat from one country to another, but we only have to consider the nature of children's games throughout the world, to realize that the childhood instincts of imitation is a universal asset.

> See, at his feet, some little plan or chart,
> Some fragments from his dream of human life
> Shaped by himself with newly-learned art;
>   A wedding or a festival,
>   A mourning or a funeral. . . .

WORDSWORTH : Ode on the Intimations of Immortality

Language as we have seen adds a considerable element of complexity to drama, and a good deal of groundwork can be done without language, by miming. A class should preferably be taken outside the classroom to somewhere with room both for movement and for 'spectating'. The work may begin by asking students to demonstrate how they think a blind man, a cripple, a soldier, a king, a giant, or an old man would walk across the acting area; their attempts might be discussed, and perhaps improved. The next stage might be to suggest work situations in which students are asked to mime the activities of farmers, porters, carpenters, typists, weavers, blacksmiths, mechanics and so on. In all these activities a competitive, or perhaps better a puzzle element can be introduced; for example the teacher can instruct students individually, who then have to perform their mime well enough for the rest of the class to guess what they are representing. Later, more complex situations can be thought out, sometimes by the teacher, sometimes by students themselves, requiring more developed action; for example, a thief creeps up to a house, carefully breaks his way in, searches until he finds a locked box, carries it away triumphantly, only to open it later and find that it is empty; or, a group of travellers making their way through thick forest find their progress barred by a deep swift river, so they chop down and trim several tree trunks to form an improvised bridge. At a later stage, miming can be used to accompany and illustrate stories and poems: some members of a class reading aloud, while others perform the actions being referred to, or implied.

At a certain point, the introduction of speech must be attempted; and here again, moving from the simple towards the more complex, it is probably advisable to work first from simple texts. Suitable ones can be found in dramatic poems, where the rhythmic arrangement of the language can be a great help towards the production of lively, authentic speech. At first the dramatized element might be quite small in relation to the narrative, as in the well-known poem 'The Blind Man and the Elephant'; and later it could occupy a much greater proportion of the whole, as in the ballad 'O, Where have you been, Lord Randal my son?' Teachers will help students to find suitable scenes for dramatizing from well-known stories, or from current class readers; sometimes dialogue will already be available in the stories, sometimes it will not be difficult for students to extemporize and develop hints given in the original. The time will come for students to invent dramatic situations and sketches of their own, and teachers can often help by providing outline suggestions (e.g. 'Lost and Found'; 'Snatching Success out of apparent Failure'; 'Unmasking an Impostor'; 'The Biter Bit' and so on), leaving students to interpret the suggestion according to their own imaginations. Judicious licence may be given to students who have some idea of being satirical, as the satirical spirit is very closely related with shrewd observations. In particular, stories and myths belonging to students' own cultures will usually prove very fruitful sources of material. Students should not be expected to do *too much* at first; it is more important for them to learn how to build up a dramatic situation with clearly defined characters grouped around a strong dramatic crisis, than to fill whole exercise books with rambling dialogue which lacks any unity of theme or action.

Teachers should consider how dramatic activities of the above kinds can be socialized in a school: what begins in the classroom can be extended to provide entertainments to other classes, at Saturday-night parties, Open Days and so on. Area drama festivals of course can be very helpful in promoting serious enthusiasm, while the annual School Play, often regarded as one of the highlights of the school year, also has its place, more especially if it is the culmination of a good deal of dramatic work at lower levels. Full notice should also be taken of local dramatic activities outside the school, and students should be encouraged to draw these into their school work when possible – these might include drumming, masks, traditional dancing, or puppetry. Such forms of socialization are strong incentives, and also encourage students to aim at the best possible standard of performance.

Elaborate staging and properties are not always necessary to stimulate dramatic activities, but it is useful to build up a kind of property box containing a few rudimentary items, odd bits of cloth for cloaks; lengths of wood for swords, daggers, sceptres; cardboard crowns and so on. The dramatist's chief, and unendingly varied, resource is of course the human body and its resources for expressive action. The teacher should always be ready to give a lead, knowing that, once their imaginations have been fired, his students can be depended upon to be endlessly inventive.

When a tradition of dramatic activity on these lines has been developed in a school, the job of studying and interpreting the great masterpieces will present far fewer problems.

Shakespeare

The study of Shakespeare is sometimes a matter of controversy, especially where English is not the students' first language. Some sceptics regard the endurance of Shakespeare into the twentieth century chiefly as a result of the flourishing Stratford-on-Avon 'Shakespeare industry'. On the other hand, Shakespeare seems to have an increasing body of sincere admirers, spread throughout the English-speaking world. There is no doubt that the language of his plays can be difficult, but these difficulties are also experienced by most students for whom English is the mother tongue, and Shakespeare is very rarely studied in English schools before the upper classes of secondary schools. Many of the difficulties spring less from the basic patterns of the language than from the unexpected nature of the ideas expressed, and grappling with these is an important part of the educational process. Occasional difficulties arising from the archaisms, witticisms, unexpected metaphors and extravagant hyperboles do occur, but, as Edward Sapir, the great linguistic philosopher, has said:

It is not the least likely that a truly great style can seriously oppose itself to the basic form patterns of the language. It not only incorporates them, it builds on them. The merit of such a style is that it does with ease and economy what the language is always trying to do.

(*Language*, 1921)

Shakespeare, in other words, although composing his plays over four hundred years ago, was using essentially the same English language that we all use today. Sitting in a theatre (or a cinema) watching a play by Shakespeare, one very quickly loses any sense of struggling with a strange language; the scenes, the characters, the situations seem to speak to us directly, vindicating the comment by Shakespeare's friend and professional rival that 'he was not of an age, but for all time'.

There are other reasons why Shakespeare is still found in school and college syllabuses. So many of his plays, the situations in them, the characters, the speeches, even many of the individual phrases, like the King James translation of the Bible, form part of the cultural background of the English Language. If the language is at times difficult, the situations in the plays themselves, lying so near to the consciousness of universal modern man, are strong enough to carry the average student over quite a number of language problems. At the same time, the study of a Shakespeare play must be approached with an intelligent wariness, and teachers must be alert to the kinds of help which students may need; the use of an appropriate edition (such as the New Swan Edition) can do much to lighten such labours as are necessary.

There are many other dramatists of note, including some whose works have been translated into English from other languages, who will repay study. Special attention, perhaps, should be given to original plays written in English by dramatists who themselves have English as a second language, and are therefore able to make authentic use of the styles of English current in their own country. While the author of this book recalls highly successful performances by African students of such masterpieces of world drama as Sophocles' *Antigone*, Aristophanes' *Lysistrata*, Shakepeare's *Macbeth*, Ibsen's *Peer Gynt*, Synge's *Playboy of the Western World*, he recalls as no less worth while, and highly appropriate to the performers, Wole Soyinka's *Swamp-Dwellers*. Soyinka's dramatic successes point to infinite possibilities of future development.

Demonstration

We shall now consider, as a practical example, how a teacher might set about dealing with the short play *Born to Die* by Sam Tulya-Muhika, which is published in *Short East African Plays in English* (Edited by Cook & Lee, Heinemann, 1968). The procedure can still be shown to fall into the sequence for the 'general approach' set out in Chapter 4.

1. Preliminary assessment. Yes, this seems to offer a number of advantages. It has a fresh approach to the eternal confrontation of the old and the new: yet there are important points of conflict between the representatives of 'the new' (Stella and Dehota). The play centres around four main characters, but gives opportunities for larger numbers to join in at various points. Language? – fairly uncomplicated – normal usage, but with interesting touches of local colour (learned from Achebe?). The feelings to be expressed are strong, clearly defined: there are opportunities for bold, decisive acting, which could be done experimentally in mime, and later with words. Not a play of great literary merit, perhaps – though it has its moments. Could well be used for practical work in drama; probably most suitable for a class of mixed students, about 3rd or 4th year of the secondary school – or for older students working independently.

2. Practical decisions. Unlikely that any professional recordings of this are available, so a class will have to 'go it alone'. All the same, if they carry it through towards a final public performance, it wouldn't be too difficult to get a model reading recorded on tape. How do we approach it? – First, I think, we should get a good grasp on what the play is about – understand it rather as though it were a story; perhaps, look at a few of the more subtle points of significance, then proceed quite quickly to an appraisal in terms of dramatic performance. This will involve not so much Who stands Where? or When does she move Where? but questions such as What impression do we have of such-and-such a character? What feeling is being expressed *here*? What actions are implied in the words spoken *there*? What kind of sections (if any) does the play fall into? Where exactly do the high points, the climaxes, come? Are they conveyed in words or in actions? . . . or in both? What effects (scenery, lighting, noises, music) could help to increase the dramatic impact of the play?

3. Introduction and 4. Presentation. Can best be done for a whole class by an initial private reading, followed by questions and discussion. If the teacher is still not very confident in the class's ability some of the following questions might be given in advance as points to look for; they could also be better used to introduce discussion of the general outline of the play as soon as possible after the initial reading:

(*a*) Why are the two sister fortune-tellers living alone in the bush?
(*b*) Who is their first visitor? What kind of person is she?
(*c*) Why has she come to have her fortune told?
(*d*) How far are the sisters able to satisfy her?
(*e*) Who is the second visitor? What do we learn about him? Why is he a fugitive? What has he come to find out?
(*f*) Why are the sisters terrified when they learn his real identity?
(*g*) What crimes is he accused of?
(*h*) What does he gain from his visit to the sisters?
(*i*) What interrupts the fortune-telling session?
(*j*) What happens to the fortune-tellers?
(*k*) What is Dehota's final decision about Stella?
(*l*) What brings the play to an end?

After this introductory fact-finding inquisition, the class will obviously be in fair possession of the play, at least in broad outline. The teacher might next decide to arrange a class-reading, as a preliminary to a further stage of discussion and study, and students should be allowed further private time to prepare for this. So that the first public reading shall be as effective as possible, the teacher should choose the best readers available, having regard to the types of characters concerned; he will attempt to foresee any scenes about which special arrangements need to be made in order to avoid a ludicrous break-down (e.g. the crowd scene in *Born to Die*). Most important of all he will appoint a narrator, possibly himself, who understands the play well enough not only to read out the author's stage directions but also to extemporize if necessary to describe the situation at any point more vividly.

At a first class-reading, however conscientiously prepared, it is quite likely that there will be occasional imperfections – sentences incorrectly phrased, words mis-pronounced or mis-stressed, wrong intonations, climaxes missed and so on. The reading should not be interrupted for the correction of these, but the teacher would tacitly note them for attention at a later stage of study if they recur: in fact many of them will be eliminated automatically as the teacher will introduce the correct forms in the subsequent discussion.

5. Discussion. After the second reading, as described above, the class will probably be in a position to discuss many more detailed aspects of the play, and questions of a more searching type will encourage insight into the meaning and implication of various speeches, the feelings which lie behind them, the interdependence of word and action ('Suit the action to the word, the word to the action', as Hamlet said to his favourite players), the attitude of one character to another, the emergence of general themes, and so on. At all stages discussion will be controlled as necessary by reference to the actual text.

The following might be a possible sequence of questions for such detailed discussion of *Born to Die*:

(*a*) What do the two opening speeches suggest to us
   (i) about the powers of the sisters?
   (ii) about what is to happen in the play?
(*b*) What does Ayeri mean when she says 'Why do you tempt us to death?' (page 2, line 12).
(*c*) From Stella's conversation with the sisters (pages 2–3), what do we learn about the general situation in the country? Does it seem to be any country in particular? or is it non-specific?
(*d*) Does it seem likely that the three fortune-tellers who had previously been killed were really responsible for what they had been accused of (page 3, lines 5–11)?
(*e*) What is the system by which Layeri and Ayeri attempt to foretell the future (pages 4–5)?
(*f*) What is significant about the opening speech of the second visitor (page 6)?
(*g*) 'You killed me' (page 6, line 30). In what sense does Stella mean this. What seems to be Dehota's attitude towards her? Does it change during the course of the play?

(*h*) In what ways is Dehota a disillusioned man (page 7)?

(*i*) Why does Layeri refer to him as an '*innocent* murderer' (page 8, line 13)?

(*j*) Why does Dehota prevent the sisters from running away (pages 8–9)?

(*k*) 'You must die to live' (page 12, line 13). What does Layeri mean by this?

(*l*) What does the fall of the cowries (p. 12) seem to indicate?

(*m*)Why does Layeri ask to see Dehota's hands (page 12)? Why is he reluctant to show them?

(*n*) Which words express the violence of the crowd
  (i) on their first entry?
  (ii) after the killing of the sisters?

(*o*) 'Are you the judges and the hangman too?' (page 15, line 23). What wisdom does Dehota seem belatedly to have learned, by the time he speaks these words?

(*p*) 'But I am a woman' (page 16, line 13). How do Stella's words, feelings and actions throughout the play emphasize this statement?

(*q*) Explain the thoughts and feelings which run through Dehota's mind during his final soliloquy (page 17), especially at the words 'I can see countless eyes looking for me – not to see me, but to see my guilt' (lines 14–15), and 'Wherever I go I find problems. Is it possible that I am the problem?' (lines 20–21).

(*r*) What does the play as a whole *prove*? What is/are its message/s? Look carefully at page 11. Also compare the behaviour of the crowd (page 14), and the police (page 17). Notice that in his final speech Dehota expects to be killed by the police: is this what *we* are to suppose? or does Dehota still see in others the violence that has been in himself?

(*s*) What do you notice about the *construction* of this play? (The events referred to in the play stretch over almost the whole lifetime of Stella and Dehota; yet by setting the play at a suitable moment of climax, and by a skilful and gradual disclosure of past events in the course of the dialogue, a good effect of power and concentration is obtained.)

The teacher will not of course grimly make his way through these questions from A to Z, but use them (and any other subsidiary ones which occur to him in response to his students' answers) for a comprehensive, connected investigation of what happens in the play and of what it all means.

6. Reinforcement. Some of the more usual types of reinforcement could be used at this point, e.g. research into related topics; written accounts of the play, either objectively, or from selected view-points; exercises in writing dialogue, or further playlets; inventing stories suitable for dramatization, etc.

The characteristic form of reinforcement for a play is obviously to prepare it for *acting* which will compel students to translate it from a printed text into a three-dimensional action, in which attention must necessarily be given to many points of detail which might otherwise be passed over. How far a teacher will go with the staging of a performance must depend on many factors especially (*a*) the amount of time he has available, and (*b*) the experience and skill his students already have in practical drama. Anyway, further steps towards the realization of *Born to Die* might proceed somewhat as follows:

Further discussion in the classroom, based on study of the text, but supplemented by practical demonstration of selected episodes. The following problems might be discussed and demonstrated experimentally:

(*a*) What actions are the sisters performing before and during their two opening speeches?

(*b*) How do you think Stella would make her first appearance on the stage on page 2, and Dehota on page 6?

(*c*) Picture and represent the behaviour of the four actors on stage at the moment (page 8) when Dehota reveals his identity.

(*d*) What would Stella be doing between the remarks on page 13 'I can hear a noise' (line 11) and 'People!' (line 22)?

(*e*) How exactly would the various members of the crowd introduce their short speeches (page 14)? Need it be only the men in the crowd who speak? Can individual members of the crowd invent additional speeches?

(*f*) How should Dehota's final soliloquy be spoken, so that words, pauses, movements, etc. all seem to reflect the mixed feelings then in his mind?

(*g*) What are the 'stylized movements' of the police intended to convey, and what might these movements actually consist of?

Practical work. After the foregoing discussion, a normal class will very likely be eager to get to work, and it would be advisable to exploit this enthusiasm by taking the class to a suitable acting area (School Hall, or open field) and allowing them to act, perhaps only in mime to begin with, some of the more dramatic scenes of the play, such as the first arrival of the angry crowd, their return after the murder of the sisters, or the arrival of the police closing in upon Dehota. A good way of involving all members of a class, is to divide them into groups of 8–10 students, and ask each group to practise and then perform its own version of given scenes before the others. This would undoubtedly stimulate a good deal of thought, suggestion and experiment.

Practical Preparation of the Text. If a satisfactory standard of performance is to be arrived at, and any possible future audience genuinely entertained, the teacher has to take his performers back to the text and prepare it for memorizing. Before he allows any of his performers to memorize any of the speeches, the teacher must ensure that the performers know exactly how each word, each phrase, each speech should be delivered. This involves attention on the one hand to such things as pronunciation, stress, intonation, phrasing; on the other hand, to expression, speed – and even silence (sometimes the most intensely dramatic moments in the performance of a play are those in which nothing whatever is being spoken). Teachers of drama may well wish to make use of some of the signs and symbols used by teachers of spoken language (they will often combine the two roles) to indicate stress, intonation and rhythm; often also some of the symbols used in musical notation can be very useful, especially to indicate pauses, – ⌒ ; rests ||-|| ; crescendoes ⋖;

and diminuendoes ⋗. Underlining is perhaps the clearest way of indicating stressed syllables, and double underlining for those which require special emphasis. Much laborious groundwork is necessary at this stage, but it will have been well worth while later on in actual performance, when the play is heard to 'ring true'.

Consider, for example, the following short excerpts from *Born to Die*, to which have been added some markings which might help performers to learn a suitable declamation.

(*a*) from p. 2.

Layeri: Yes⌒ they were run down by a mob,⌒ driven by a madman　[mædmn] –

⌒a man by the name of Dehota　⌒　who called himself

a reformer.

Ayeri: He incited the mob;⌒ he got them drunk with rage for

murder;⌒ he filled them with words,⌒ with emptiness,⌒

with the opium of society.

Layeri: They were gripped by mass drunkenness;⌒so they went

out⌒to loot, to pillage, to murder,⌒to destroy. . . .　[piliðʒ]
　　　　　　　　　　　　　　　　　　　　　　　　　　[distrɔi]

(*b*) from p. 6.

Stella: Oh Maathi, I felt lonely. I felt lost. My life had no bearings　[bɛəriŋz]

without you. I wanted to know⌒whether there was a future

for us together. No-one would tell me. So I came here.

Oh⌒please⌒don't leave me. Don't throw me to life⌒all by

myself. Life is a ravenous lion without you. It's a　starved　[rævnəs]

cormorant;⌒it will devour me.⌒You killed me:　don't kill

me again.

Besides the appropriate speaking of individual lines, the teacher has to consider the structure of the play as a whole and decide which are the points of special climax which need to be brought out by proper use of emphasis, change of tempo, use of pauses, etc. For example, in *Born to Die*, the principal moments of climax appear to be as follows:

p. 3 All I want is my fortune told (*line* 16)
p. 4 I swear, I swear, by the moon, by the sun, and by the heavens (*lines* 6–7)
p. 6 Oh, you crush my hopes (*line* 3)
p. 8 But I am Dehota – Maathi Dehota! (*line* 17)
p. 11 But you cannot save people unless you understand them (*lines* 20–21)
p. 12 All went, leaving me a traveller in this trackless desert (*lines* 19–20)
p. 13 It's the crowd, the witch-hunters! (*line* 27)
p. 16 You couldn't go alone: you wouldn't be complete. Part of you is here. (*lines* 21–22)
p. 17 You're too late. I am not much to kill: I've spent my life dying. (*lines* 25–26).

The class teacher has a considerable problem to deal with in keeping a whole class occupied while this work is being done. The best thing is for him to avoid any final casting at this stage, and give every member of the class a particular principal part to study, so that in the end there will be perhaps 5 or 6 complete casts available. He must be ready himself to demonstrate exactly how he thinks each speech ought to be said, though if he can incorporate alternative versions suggested by his students so much the better. When the whole text has been prepared in this way, the process of memorizing can begin; it can be helped by various kinds of preliminary rehearsal, though these should if possible always be listened to by someone who is critical, and who will see that memorizing does not destroy the dramatic quality of the words being learned.

Business. The spoken text of a play is fundamental, but of almost equal importance are the actions and movements which accompany it. The producer should have a preliminary plan in mind as to where each character stands (or sits) on the stage, where he enters, how he may change his position during the course of a scene, what actions or gestures he should perform, when special effects should be brought in, and so on. Probably the best time to introduce these into the developing play is in the early stage of verbal rehearsal, before performers have discarded their copies of the text, so that they can make notes of where they should enter, where they should stand, how, when and where they should move, etc.

In later stages of rehearsal words and actions can then be integrated and the performance then becomes steadily more life-like.

Performance. Sooner or later the teacher has to decide what kind of final performance he is going to aim at, and there are many different ways in which drama can be realized before an audience, big or small.

At the one extreme is the full-scale School Play, performed before parents, staff, other schools, the press, local dignitaries and so on. If he is committed to this kind of performance (and there is no reason why he occasionally should not be), the teacher becomes much more of a producer, finds himself selecting only the best actors, giving them special training, and attempting to keep other members of his class involved as crowd members, noises off, or by giving them responsibilities for making properties, painting scenery, devising publicity, carrying chairs, and so on. . . .

There is much to be said, however, for the type of performance almost at the opposite extreme, which is often referred to as a workshop production. This does not aim at the completeness of a professional production. It makes little use of special costume, elaborate scenery, or detailed realistic effects; the performers may be discreetly carrying their texts in one hand, to refer to if occasionally they falter in their lines. All the same, even with such concessions to reality, amazingly life-like, sensitive and intelligent studies of a play can be given. Performances of this kind can be used to encourage full appreciation of almost all the essential elements of a dramatic performance.

8

Occasional Literature

English literature, whatever sort of appearance it makes in the handbooks and histories, developed in a hopelessly irregular way. It was written by parsons, civil servants, doctors, schoolmasters, people of all trades....

The Speaking Oak, JAMES REEVES.

Tidy-minded people tend to divide literature, as we have so far done in this book, into the *genres* of Poetry, Prose Fiction, and Drama. Now, while there is abundant material for study at all levels in those three sectors, of the total field, a great deal of valuable literature has been produced in between the standard categories. Many busy writers and thinkers, with urgent ideas and messages to communicate, have made use of the most direct form of communication. We are thinking not of entirely technical and theoretical publication in the various fields of knowledge directed chiefly to specialists, but of the vast body of 'occasional' (i.e. written for special occasions) literature produced for the man-in-the-street.

The importance of this is becoming increasingly recognized. Many people, looking back on the books which have deeply influenced them in the course of their own emotional and intellectual development, readily admit that quite a proportion of them come from the 'in between' categories. Many academic authorities have recognized this, too; for example, Professor Helen Gardner, in her Inaugural Lecture as Professor of Literature at Oxford recently referred to the danger of 'an over-emphasis on works of the imagination and a neglect of the literature of argument, persuasion, edification and polemic – of works written out of a passionate concern with great human issues'. No matter what the form, anything written from the author's sense of involvement in 'great human issues' and meaningful to the average reader's own experience of life must be allowed a place in the field of significant literature. Imagination and insight, after all, are not the special prerogatives of the restricted number of writers who prefer to use the traditional literary forms: they belong to all who can see significance in the varying situations of human life, and can put words together in any way which conveys that significance effectively.

We think first of the various kinds of periodical journalism – and we need not reserve this term only for purposes of abuse – to which many notable writers have turned, and still do. Collections of articles, essays and reviews often provide a convenient and comprehensive insight into an author's whole work and outlook, as can be illustrated in George Orwell's *Essays*, D. H. Lawrence's *Assorted Articles*, E. M. Forster's *Abinger Harvest*, G. B. Shaw's *Prefaces*, and more recently, from the developing societies, Tai Solarin's *Thinking with You*, or Niraud Chaudhuri's *Passage to England*.

Having once ventured this far, we shall find it difficult to deny that very often

Biographies and Autobiographies must be recognized as literature. For example, *The Life of Helen Keller*, Axel Munthe's *The Story of San Michele*, Kenyatta's *No Picnic on Mount Kenya*, Mphahlele's *Down Second Avenue*, Abrahams' *Tell Freedom, Equiano's Travels*. These might lead us to look at such things as Letters, Diaries and Chronicles, where again we are likely to find notable documents of unfailing human interest. And finally we may discover that quite a number of what may seem at first to be technical works of science, history, religion, politics, sociology, arts and crafts, have been conceived and written in such a way as to bring them into the realms of literature: for example, Gilbert White's *Natural History of Selbourne*, Izaak Walton's *Compleat Angler*, Darwin's *Voyage of the Beagle*, Sturt's *Wheelwright's Shop*, H. G. Wells' *Short History of the World*, C. H. Waddington's *The Scientific Attitude*, van der Post's *Lost World of the Kalahari*, or John Berger's *A Fortunate Man*.

We are not of course advocating that the whole of a literature course should be occupied with the study of such works but a proportion of them can add variety, as well as remind us, and our students, once again that literature is something we do expect to be connected significantly with the problems and experiences of ordinary people. Some teachers of literature would even go so far as to say that no course of literature could be complete without at least some introduction to works of these kinds.

Not *all* books of a non-literary character merit inclusion, and it may indeed be difficult in some circumstances to decide where to draw the line, especially if for example there might be a wish to study the biography or the thoughts of an important political leader. It should be possible to apply some simple tests in cases of doubt. Can we say that any non-literary book under consideration for inclusion in a literature course should have the following characteristics?

(*a*) It should bear the distinct stamp of the personality of its author. (This would rule out standard textbooks.)
(*b*) It should employ language with some degree of skill, at the very least of clarity, and possibly also of distinction.
(*c*) It should provide honest, undistorted human experience likely to be of genuine interest to the student. (This would rule out works of stereotyped propaganda, whether religious or political.)

From their very nature, of course, books in this category are more likely to be of interest to students at more mature stages, as may be deduced from Chapter 3.

How are such books to be studied? It seems unnecessary to elaborate at great length on this, after all that has been said so far, for the teacher should have no difficulty in adapting the methods of study recommended for the orthodox categories, particularly for prose fiction. It will of course be relevant to consider carefully the actual circumstance under which each book was written, and the particular purpose which the author may have had in mind. Otherwise our basic approach needs little modification. As always, the aim of study will be to elicit whatever the author intended to put into his book, whether in the form of events, characters, techniques, thoughts or feelings, or whatever combination of these the book contains; and the same sorts of aids to study are likely to be appropriate and possible.

Let us suppose, for the purposes of demonstration that the teacher has recently come across *Equiano's Travels*, the abridgment of a work first published in London in 1789 under the formidable title of *The Interesting Narrative of the Life of Olaudah Equiano, or Gustavus Vassa the African, written by himself*, and recently re-edited by Paul Edwards in Heinemann's *African Writers Series*. Is this a work, he asks, that could be brought into the literature course? 'Equiano did not claim to be a literary artist' he may see in the Editor's Introduction (p. xvi) – How does he decide whether this can come within the scope of 'literature'? It is useful to bear in mind a saying by one of the leading novelists of our own century (D. H. Lawrence) – 'We judge a work of literature by its effect on our sincere and vital emotions'. So the teacher must read the work, judging it first of all by its effect on himself and then considering whether it is likely to have a similar effect on his students. Are there any linguistic or cultural difficulties? If so, will the interest of the narrative itself carry students over all obstacles? What is the best method of study for this particular book? What other kind of activities can be based on it?

Firstly, the teacher is likely to note, this is a book of particular interest – one of the first accounts written by an African who had travelled extensively (even if not entirely voluntarily) outside Africa. The author had been in a position from which to report on some of the great historic processes affecting the relationship between the 'older' and the 'newer' nations. He had passed through a wide range of experiences, involving despair, hope, fear, admiration; he had gone a long way to assimilating a culture other than his own; he had learned to sail a ship, travelled to the Arctic regions and eventually married an Englishwoman. In fact the range of experiences recorded in this work give it very special educational value. In the new abridged edition there is a considerable amount of useful material in the shape of historic illustrations, Appendices and Notes which throw additional light on the narrative itself.

How could the study of the book be organized? There would be perhaps two stages of study. Firstly a fairly quick reading through the whole, dividing the fourteen chapters into perhaps five assignments, each tested or encouraged by short factual tests or quizzes. Secondly a selection of topics for more special study in the form of essays, reports, diagrams, requiring careful re-reading, selection and further research. The teacher might indicate a whole range of possibilities such as the following, and expect each student to attempt one:

(a) *Anthropological.* What picture is given of tribal life as recalled by Equiano in the Kingdom of Benin two hundred and fifty years ago? How does it compare with students' memories of their own childhood? What comparisons could be made with Achebe's *Things Fall Apart*?

(b) *Historical.* What historical events and processes were taking place during Equiano's lifetime? In Africa? In Britain? In America? How do these events affect his narrative?

(c) *Geographical.* Where did his travels actually take him? Follow them with the help of an atlas, and plot them on a sketch-map adding significant details at each point.

(d) *Technical.* What do we learn from the story about ships, seamanship, navigation, naval warfare in the eighteenth century? What about trade, commerce, and finance?

(e) *Social.* What kind of impression does the author give of Slavery, especially the Atlantic Slave Trade? What were its essential evils? Show how these are feelingly represented.

(f) *Speculative.* What is the relationship between Slavery and the more modern problem of Racial Prejudice? Why was Equiano always glad to return to Britain from the West Indies? (cf. 'I had thought only slavery dreadful, but the state of a free negro appeared to me now even worse' – p. 84).

(g) *Psychological.* Examine the stages by which Equiano assimilated himself to western customs and techniques. What were some of his early mistakes? What kind of standing did he achieve in the end?

(h) *Literary.* Which passages stand out particularly, for demonstrating the author's graphic ability with the English Language? (e.g. the Sea Battle, Chapter V; the Shipwreck in the Bahamas, Chapter X; etc.).

(i) *Practical.* Explain precisely the predicament of Mr Mondle (pages 51–52). Use a diagram to show exactly what happened. Compare with the situation of James Wait in Conrad's *Nigger of the Narcissus*.

(j) *Inductive.* A more sophisticated exercise would be to assess the evidence brought by the Editor (pages xv–xvi) to prove that the text as originally printed was the unaided work of Equiano himself.

Another type of work for which *Equiano's Travels* would seem very suitable (though here we are anticipating Chapter 9) would be to provide opportunities for students' own original writing or imaginative composition. The book contains plenty of characters and episodes which are only lightly sketched in and which could be expanded. There are episodes in Equiano's life which we don't learn a great deal about in the book itself, but seem fascinating to speculate more about, for example, his experience as Commissary for Stores to the expedition for the settlement of Poor Blacks in Sierra Leone in 1787 (see Appendix I).

Then also a study of *Equiano's Travels* could well be linked up with other books, obviously enough with accounts of other early travels in Africa or in other parts of the world. Some of the experiences described in the *Travels* might well lead to the reading of such expressions of racial disharmony as James Baldwin's *The Fire Next Time*, while a comparison with Daniel Defoe would obviously suggest reading works by him, not only *The Adventures of Robinson Crusoe* (which would no doubt already be familiar), but also perhaps that most vivid piece of reporting (another famous piece of occasional literature) the *Journal of the Plague Year*.

So, with any other pieces of occasional literature, the teacher would make his appreciation, and then his plan of operation.

9

The Link with Composition

This book is principally concerned with the teaching and study of Literature, but we have recognized from the beginning that there is no hard and fast division between Literature and Language. In fact many teachers of English, or other languages, will nearly always find that they have the twofold responsibility of extending their students' capacity for self-expression, as well as introducing them to the literature written in a language. It is always likely that courses in language (for example, all those leading to the General Certificate of Education, various School Certificates, and their equivalents), whatever other activities may be included, will always require students to develop their ability in various forms of 'extended expression', or Composition; and each year's work will include quite a number of assignments of this kind. Good composition, the building up of fluent, sustained and organized expression, must be related to students' own interests and experiences. So, in recent years there has been a move away from the more abstract and speculative topics which used to be customary (such as 'Islands', 'Friendship', etc.) and the introduction of others which need to be answered from students' personal observations and experiences (such as 'Describe a journey which you remember well', 'Give an account of a typical wedding, funeral, or coming of age, as celebrated in your own locality'). This change of emphasis has undoubtedly led to a great deal of more honest, purposeful, and *better* writing than the older approach – and incidentally has made the task of teachers in reading students' compositions a good deal more interesting!

If it is agreed that composition should be based on experience, let us pause for a moment to consider what this involves. 'Experience' – 'the name men give to their mistakes', as one cynic has put it – is essentially something which takes place in the mind, the process of assimilation and comparison which goes on in each one of us as things happen – as we absorb new events, processes, ideas, sensations, people, into our existing consciousness. Obviously enough, a good deal of experience comes to us from the actual circumstances of our life in the world of time and space; but, just as obviously, if we think for a moment, we absorb a good deal also from the world of the imagination, from the works of literature we study (as well as from other subjects in the curriculum). One of the most instinctive ways in which we express our delight in a piece of literature is by saying that it is 'life-like', and indeed all those people whose culture includes access to a literature of any significance can be said to some extent to 'live' in the literature they know (though this can have its dangers if taken to extremes).

When searching for topics for students' composition exercises, teachers may very legitimately look in the literature currently being studied; an imaginative selection of tasks for written work will increase not only students' insight into literature but also to their skill and resourcefulness in language.

Let us review some of the ways in which composition work can be based on literature. Once again we have to remember the principle of grading, and try always to devise exercises which match students' psychological and linguistic maturity at any time.

1. Retelling a story. Story-telling is one of the most ancient and respected customs in all societies, and most students who have enjoyed a good story will be very ready to retell it, either verbally or in writing, and teachers should exploit this readiness. Students' inherent satisfaction in retelling stories can be developed if the teacher sometimes *leads* them, to make sure that the whole experience has been grasped (How does it all begin? Then what happens? And what does that lead to? But why exactly does . . .? And what is the result of that? . . . And how does it all end? And what does that signify? . . . etc.). Some teachers may feel that the mere retelling of stories is a rather slavish, mechanical exercise, but there can surely be much value in it, even at quite advanced levels, especially if students are encouraged not only to recount the basic facts of the story, but to bring to life the feelings and relationships of the characters, and to indicate the spirit and atmosphere of the story as a whole or in its various parts (e.g. whether of curiosity, amazement, familiarity, fear, suspense, scorn, mystery, joy, relief). In fact, students should feel that a re-telling of the story, is in fact a full and faithful *re*-creation of it.

This raises the question of how independent students should be in their expression when retelling stories. If we assume that they are learners of the language, as well as enjoyers of the literature, we shall not mind if they re-use a good deal of the actual vocabulary, phraseology and dialogue of the original. The only proviso is that this language must be genuinely recalled, and not just copied (either orally or in writing) from a textbook. In the earlier stages, particularly, it is a good thing for there to be a good deal of oral work – recounting and discussing the story, before any move is made towards writing.

When the stories being used are longer, and students more mature, re-telling could be limited to particular parts of the story, specific chapters or episodes of novels; for example, What did Kwase do at Accra? (Duodu, *The Gab Boys*); What happened to Titus Obi at the Igbetti Rest House? (Aluko, *Kinsman and Foreman*). Describe how Pip met his unknown bene-factor. (Dickens, *Great Expectations*, Chapter 39)

It should be noted that the activity of retelling a story need not be based only on works which are themselves written in the form of prose fiction. Many poems and plays have an element of narrative in their structure which can very usefully be brought out by retelling. This is quite obvious in poems such as Coleridge's *Ancient Mariner*, but would also apply to some extent to Keats' *Ode to a Nightingale*. (Where does the poem open? What is the poet doing? How does he feel? Then what happens? What effect does this have?) The suitability of the method for dealing with plays is equally marked, and students could be asked to explain what happens in Act I of *Richard II*, or to outline the story of *The Swamp Dwellers* (Soyinka). When retelling the story element found in poems or plays, students would of course be permitted to use a normal prose form of narrative, though they might be praised if they were able to incorporate some of the more significant phrases of the original in their own versions.

2. Retelling a story – from a fresh angle. So far we have been thinking of the retelling of stories from the point of view embodied in the original. It is an excellent exercise of the imagination – and of the language skills – to retell a story from a fresh point of view. The simplest example of this would be to take a story told in the third person (he) and to imagine how the central character (or any other) would narrate it himself, i.e. in the first person. The techniques of shifting view-points has been used by many distinguished writers, and always has the effect of stimulating the imagination and enabling us to see a character or a situation in much greater depth. Used as a teaching exercise, it has the value of requiring students to take careful note of the actual data of the story, so that their own contributions and adaptations convincingly match the authentic version. For example, students might be asked to give some account of the events of *Robinson Crusoe* as seen by Man Friday. They would need, to begin with, to make a close examination of the actual text to see what hints it has to give on such topics as where Man Friday came from, what first brought him to the island, his first impressions on seeing Robinson Crusoe, their first attempts to communicate, their subsequent relationship, and so on. . . . Similarly students could be asked to imagine how Obierika in Achebe's *Things Fall Apart* would describe the career of Okonkwo; how Greta in Conton's *The African* would describe (perhaps in a personal diary) her relationship with Kisimi Kamara; how Louisa Gradgrind (in Dickens' *Hard Times*) would give an account of the upbringing which led to her surprising marriage with Mr Bounderby; or how Macduff might give an account of the events leading to the enthronement of Macbeth as King of Scotland.

The same technique could also be applied to poems and plays, the fresh view-point again being expressed in prose. For example, it would be interesting to have the commentary of Ocol (Okot p'Bitek's *Song of Lawino*) upon his wife and the traditional way of life after his return to his homeland; or to imagine Kongi (Soyinka's *Kongi's Harvest*) giving an intelligent account of his plans for the economic and political development of his country of Isma.

3. Imaginary episodes. As a development from the previous type of exercise, students can be invited to imagine and describe new episodes to fit into existing stories. A useful way of introducing this kind of exercise is to suggest that they have discovered a chapter of the original book which was lost in the post, or in the publisher's office. This exercise, if carried out successfully, has several kinds of value. Firstly it encourages a disciplined use of the imagination, for the new episode is quite different from anything so far encountered in the parent story. Secondly, it requires a careful reappraisal of the original so that the events, thoughts, speeches invented can be seen to fit in consistently. (Great excitement and enthusiasm occurs when members of a class listen to each other's attempts at this exercise.) Many students may easily be able to think of new episodes to develop; if there is any uncertainty, the teacher can easily give a few suggestions. For example, Kisimi Kamara (in *The African*) when in financial difficulties in Britain might appeal for help to the British Council Representative in Edinburgh, or Njoroke (in Ngugi's *Weep Not Child*) might have an unexpected opportunity of meeting his great hero Jomo Kenyatta.

More advanced students with some degree of language sophistication might well be expected to reproduce some of the language characteristics of the original author, if these are at all distinctive. For example, the Drinkard (Tutuola, *The Palm-Wine Drinkard*) could be imagined in a new episode with the Obedient Eight Wheeled Caterpillar, or Mr Biswas (V. S. Naipaul's *The House of Mr Biswas*) might be imagined announcing to his family that he has won the Government Lottery and proposes to go into the hotel business.

There are obviously infinite opportunities for exercises in composition along these lines, the only limit being the inventiveness of the student. The disciplined element of the exercise should always be borne in mind, for the highest praise will be given only to the compositions which perfectly match the original.

4. Original writing. The sequence of suggestions in this chapter brings us fairly near to the idea of absolutely original or creative writing, which does not at first seem to have much to do with the teaching of literature. We should remember however that many of the world's greatest authors have, in their earliest days, been influenced by other authors whose works they have read. So a teacher who wishes to start his class off on original writing may wish to make considerable use of existing literature. A good way of stimulating students is to suggest a number of generalized themes, of which they can be invited to produce individual illustrations, drawing upon their personal observations and experience. It can be helpful if such themes have previously been implanted in their minds by some of the literature they have studied. For example, a theme such as 'The Abuse of Power' might be related back to Shakespeare's *Julius Caesar*; 'The Difficulty of Being Honest' to Achebe's *No Longer at Ease*; or 'The Need for Tolerance' to Davidson Nicol's story *As The Night The Day*.

5. Composition – Poetry. There is always a good deal of discussion as to when, or whether, students should be invited to attempt the writing of poetry. Some teachers, thinking of the technical difficulties of much poetry, will be hesitant to commit their students to such a dangerous task. Others will remember that in all the literatures of the world poetry has been one of the primal forms of literary expression (and not only because verse form makes for convenient memorization!), and consider it at least worth an attempt. Throughout this chapter so far, we have assumed that the majority of students' compositions will be done in prose. However, some experiments in the writing of verse can certainly be justified, not only for the sharpened observation and interest in language it can promote, but for the renewed interest it can arouse in the poems the students have to study for other reasons.

How can students best be encouraged and helped to produce their own poems? The important thing, in this as in other matters, is to work from models, and to make sure that the models are suitable for imitation! Although in their study of literature students may be dealing with poems which have quite complex metrical and rhyming schemes, for poetic composition they should be given models which do not involve too complex manipulation of language. The best poems for this purpose often consist of series of observations and statements (perhaps also occasional questions and exclamations), and belong to the tradition of Free Verse. The fact that students' experiments are not hampered by the search for rhyming words and so on, does not rule out the introduction of *comparisons* (Metaphor, as Aristotle observed thousands of years ago, is one of the basic elements of poetry); nor does it rule out all the effects which can be obtained by the use of varying and contrasted *registers* of the language. Fortunately there are plenty of poems available for study and imitation which embody these requirements. Much of the contemporary poetry of the English-speaking world in the last half century has been of this type (T. S. Eliot's *Journey of the Magi*, for example, is one of the influential poems of our times); much of it was influenced by the early Chinese poetry translated into English by Arthur Waley, and many of these poems are not at all forbidding to imitate. For example, how many poems in any country could be modelled on *The Little Cart*:

> The little cart jolting and banging through the yellow haze of dusk;
> The man pushing behind, the woman pulling in front.
> They have left the city and do not know where to go.
> 'Green, green, those elm-tree leaves: *they* will cure my hunger,
> If only we could find some quiet place to sup on them together.'

> The wind has flattened the yellow mother-wort:
> Above it in the distance they see the walls of a house.
> '*There* surely must be people living, who'll give you something to eat.'
> They tap at the door, but no one comes: they look in, but the kitchen
>   is empty.
> They stand hesitating in the lonely road and their tears fall like rain.

Many other useful models can be found in the work of poets who use English as a Second Language throughout the Commonwealth. For example, John Pepper Clark's *Night Rain* could be imitated many thousand times for its quiet recording of a commonplace experience vividly observed, and his *Ibadan* could give rise to an unlimited number of poems about places.

A good deal of the pleasure of poetry does come at times from the formal arrangements of sounds, rhythm, rhyme, verse patterns, etc., and any course of poetry reading should certainly include a good proportion of that kind. Occasionally, a student will be found who has some ability to organize language in this way, and he should be given due encouragement, but such facility cannot often be expected, and teachers should realize that much useful poetical composition can be done without it.

6. Composition – Drama. As we saw in Chapter 7, drama is one of the most difficult literary forms, for it requires perhaps a higher degree of skill in selection and organization of language and episode than any other. Nevertheless, since drama usually creates a great deal of enthusiasm, teachers of literature will occasionally wish to see what their students can do in this line. Students' struggles with problems of dramatic technique (How do the spectators know what has happened before? How can we avoid too many scene changes? How can we make it sound life-like? How can we make it *dramatic*?) will give them an increased respect for and an increased interest in the works of the acknowledged masters they may have to study.

One of the easiest ways of making a start with dramatic composition is to quarry from existing works which already embody dramatic situations and a certain amount of dramatic dialogue (Chapter 39 of *Great Expectations* is an excellent example). What is already provided usually needs a certain amount of adaptation or extension; perhaps also a certain amount of grouping with other scenes in order to produce the compact, concentrated effect of good drama.

Another method of inaugurating dramatic composition is by means of imaginary conversations, based on well-known dramatic situations. For example, a dissatisfied worker confronts a ruthless boss; a traditionally minded parent rebukes a revolutionary son; a civil servant interviews a business man; a fugitive comes for refuge to an unsympathetic host. A few snatches of conversation soon require the establishment of 'character' and reference to events, past and future, and, with mutal discussion in groups and perhaps reading or acting what is invented to other students, unpredictable results may follow.

A further method, which has some very distinguished precedents in the ranks of distinguished authors, is to glance through a newspaper, where either on the local or international scale, dramatic events are always being reported. It does not take students long to begin to imagine what might be said, for example, when a General Gowan receives a visit from an ex-President Azikiwe, or a British Prime Minister meets the Head of Government of a turbulent Ulster. And what opportunities for dramatic invention lie within a newspaper item such as the following:

Athens, August 17

A Greek doctor who, with his wife and two young sons, hijacked a Greek air liner and forced the pilot at gun and dagger point to fly them to Albania, apologized later to other passengers.

for his school certificate killed all his interest in the subject, there are many others who have found that the study opens up new horizons of experience – intellectual, emotional and linguistic. The provisos to be observed are important: firstly the detailed analysis undertaken must be relevant to a proper appreciation of the *whole*: and, secondly, the level of complexity must be related to the intellectual capacity of the students concerned.

A second objection brought against examinations in literature is that they often have the effect of restricting the range of students' reading. The need for detailed study and knowledge of a number of prescribed books discourages both teachers and students from venturing further than they absolutely have to. We have already discussed the value of both intensive and extensive reading in Chapter 6, and again we meet the familiar dilemma found in many educational processes – of striking a reasonable balance between depth and breadth. The problem presents itself in many ways – the buying of books, the apportioning of class time, the use of students' own revision time and each teacher has to make his own decisions. There is, of course, no absolute virtue in having read a large quantity of books – Who was it who wrote of

> The learned blockhead, ignorantly read,
> With loads of learned lumber in his head? –

The essential value of literary studies comes from the *quality* of reading, and the significance of the experience gained; this depends chiefly on the merit of the books selected and on the degree of insight which is gained *in* and *through* them. To read a carefully selected group of books in a given time, thoroughly and with *genuine* appreciation, is better than tearing through ten times that number without opportunity for discussion and reflection. The English tradition of literary studies has always rejected the kind of outline course, popular in some parts of the world, in which students acquire many facts about authors and works of literature without ever gaining first-hand experience of any of them.

We should remember too that examinations are devised for *students*, rather than for experts, and one of their principal aims is to train students in the *methods* of dealing with a subject. Once the training has been acquired, it can then be applied to the fullest range of materials which time and opportunity permit.

Nevertheless, while the main emphasis is on training in appreciation, a course in literature, and the examinations which go with it, ought to give students some *perspectives*, some view of the whole field which the subject comprehends, some understanding of the variety of interest and experience it offers. Do examinations, as at present available, ignore this obligation? It we look at some typical examination papers we see that they are in fact structured so that the candidate has to answer questions on, say, a Shakespeare or a modern play, a classical novel, a modern novel, and a collection of poems; and even these are to be selected from a considerably wider range offered in the syllabus. This secures some degree of variety from the beginning, but even without reference to the examination syllabus, much more can be done on the initiative of the enterprising teacher and the co-operative student. Even when a course in literature appears anchored to a certain number of prescribed books, it is possible to go beyond these, and study each one in the widest possible context in a way which will not only increase appreciation of the work itself, but will enhance the candidate's prospects of examination success. For example, if the prescribed play is G. B. Shaw's *Arms and the Man*, some further acquaintance with Shaw's plays, such as the *Doctor's Dilemma*, *The Devil's Disciple*, *The Apple Cart*, can give a fuller impression of Shaw's dramatic work in relation to the theatre for which he wrote, and the age in which he lived. If the prescribed novel is Achebe's *Arrow of God*, knowledge of his other novels, and other novels by his contemporaries, can promote a fuller appreciation even of that one.

How is such additional reading to be revealed? Some types of examination paper make definite provision for the encouragement and investigation of additional reading. Even if this is not the case, teachers can train their students to reveal their additional reading as part of the frame of reference in which they discuss the books which are set. No doubt further experiments, and techniques of examination need to be devised, and are likely to appear in coming years, to signify the importance attached to wider reading, without sacrificing the value of detailed study. There is nothing inherent in the idea of examinations in literature which positively prevents or penalizes the widest reading which teachers and students are capable of undertaking.

The third objection which we should consider is more serious. The anxiety to succeed in examinations (or the fear of failure) drives many students to examination-passing techniques which are opposed to the proper educational discipline of the subject (and the same is no doubt true of other subjects in the curriculum). Whereas the study of literature is justified by the opportunities it gives to students of grappling personally with various pieces of life-experience, in fact preparation for examinations becomes a calculated, mechanical business of spotting questions, memorizing model answers, pleasing the examiners, and so on. Instead of trying to think for themselves and working out their own responses, students ask to be told 'what they ought to say', and rely heavily on various authorities – perhaps on their own teacher, but also on many types of students' guides, some of them of very *dubious* authority. This is no new problem in examinations in literature, and is encountered as much in supposedly developed countries as anywhere else. In the famous Makerere Report *On the Teaching of English Overseas 1962*, it was said of examinations in literature that 'Nothing should be done which encourages a rehearsed response'. Nevertheless this bad tradition of the 'mechanization' of literary studies, persists, and all teachers of literature who value their subject must consider what should be done to counteract it.

What causes this frustrating falsification of the subject? To some extent it is an aspect of the highly competitive atmosphere found especially in developing countries in which there is a desperate race for qualifications conferring economic and social advantages, and applies as much to òther subjects as to Literature. As far as examinations in Literature are concerned, it may be due to a general lack of confidence on the part of students, and to some extent of teachers, who are not convinced that they can make an acceptable approach to literary works without some external guide. If works prescribed are archaic or difficult – perhaps unrelated to the social context in which they are being studied – this lack of confidence is understandable, and the situation will be improved when a better selection of texts is introduced and as the professional knowledge and competence of teachers increases. The form of examinations themselves are also partly responsible, for some types of test, especially the predictable essay question, can easily be prepared for in a mechanical way, by rote-learning. As long as examination tests are offered which can be crammed for, students cannot altogether be blamed for taking the line of least resistance. An urgent task for teachers and examiners in literature is to devise methods of testing which will circumvent the offering of rehearsed responses, and guide students back to a first-hand study of their texts. The general way to reform seems likely to be along the lines of the practical criticism associated with the name of I. A. Richards, but the problem is how to adapt those procedures to students of different ages and ability, and to apply them not only to the short 'unseen' passages which Richards used, but longer works of literature.

Before going further into the design of an acceptable examination in literature, it seems appropriate first of all to agree on what ought to be tested. What do we expect students who have pursued a course of studies in literature to have acquired in the way of knowledge, of insight, of skills? Can it be analysed in the following way? – The successful student should have acquired something in each of the following categories:

(a) *Information*: basic to the structure of the work; contained either within the work itself, or essential to its fullest understanding. What happened? Where? When? How many? Names? Dates?

(b) *Concepts*: perception of how the basic data of each work are organized. What kind of . . . .? With what effect? Why? (purpose) Why? (cause and effects) What essential problems arise? What are the factors involved in the problems?

(c) *Perspectives*: What does this signify? Of what is it typical? Where does it fit in? What conclusions do we draw? Where else could it happen? What does it mean 'for me'?

(d) *Appreciation*: both literary and linguistic. Why is it put like this (so and not otherwise)? What is the effect of this word, of that image, of this episode, of that character? What type of language is being used?

Having decided what the successful student should have acquired, the task is then to devise suitable methods for checking, or sampling, his acquisitions. Conventional methods of examining in literature have in the past included the context question, occasionally the paraphrase, occasionally the appreciation exercise, but the great weight of responsibility has fallen on the essay. We may still feel that these methods, sensibly combined and sensitively handled, may tell us all we want to know, and at the same time encourage the best possible approach to literary studies. On the other hand, in view of some of the objections considered above and a good deal of contemporary experience in testing techniques, we might at least consider whether some improvements can be made. Ought the essay, for example, in spite of its great prestige as an instrument of intellectual investigation useful in all disciplines, to be called for rather less? Could it be replaced by more specific testing techniques, related to all the various levels of appreciation on which the student is being examined?

Such problems cannot easily be considered in the abstract, and can best be evaluated from some practical proposals. Let us suppose that Class IV of a secondary school has been studying Crabbe's narrative poem *Peter Grimes*. Using conventional procedures the teacher might decide to set an assignment such as

'Write a critical appreciation of *Peter Grimes*'
or perhaps
'George Crabbe – a sentimental realist. Do you agree?'
and would not be surprised if he received in due course a set of essays full of utterances such as the following:

> As early as 1775, when Crabbe published his poem called *Inebriety*, he sounded the two notes most characteristic of all his work: realism and a steady acceptance of his own experience of life as the proper material for his poetry. . . . He has been called 'the poet of the poor' and Byron described him as
> 'Nature's sternest painter, yet her best'.
> Though he used the elegant couplets of the eighteenth century, he refused to idealize the country life he knew so well, and there is nothing of neo-classical pastoralism in his work. . . .

– which is in fact found in the Notes to one of the popular anthologies reprinting the poem.

As an alternative, after some systematic study of the poem, the resourceful teacher might prepare a series of questions on the following lines:

Test on Peter Grimes

Group 1. Information

Indicate by underlining the correct completion to each of the following statements about the poem.

    (*a*) The poem was written by:
        John Milton, Thomas Gray, George Crabbe, John Keats, Benjamin Britten.

    (*b*) It was first published in:
        1783, 1807, 1810, 1812, 1956.

    (*c*) The poem is written in:
        Blank verse, Ballad measure, Rhyming couplets, Rime royal, Iambic tetrameters.

(*d*) Peter Grimes carried out his work:
in London, in Hull, on the East Coast, at Lands End, in Wales.

(*e*) He selected his apprentices from:
the local town, Yarmouth, an orphanage, the London poor-house,
Lowestoft.

(*f*) He was forbidden to appoint any more apprentices by:
the Bishop, the women of the town, the local priest, the Chief of Police,
the Mayor.

(*g*) After the death of his apprentices he became very:
relieved, rich, careless, lonely, contented.

(*h*) The three places he always looked upon with dread were:
cold windy hills, buildings he had robbed, the site of various gallows,
places where his apprentices died, places where his ship had been
wrecked.

(*i*) Peter Grimes eventually died:
in his own home, in the church, in his boat, in the poor-house, in
prison.

Group 2. Concepts. Write a short paragraph on any *two* of the following (i.e.
about 100 words each).

(*a*) The relationship between Peter Grimes and his father.

(*b*) Peter Grimes' treatment of his apprentices.

(*c*) The relationship between Peter Grimes and the local community.

(*d*) The significance of Peter Grimes' final 'confession'.

Group 3. Perspectives. Write a paragraph on *one* of the following:

(*a*) Arrangements for social welfare in Britain at the time when *Peter
Grimes* was written.

(*b*) Crabbe's particular interests as a poet, as represented in *Peter Grimes*.

(*c*) Refer to any other works of literature which seem to you to present
comparable themes.

Group 4. Appreciation. Choose any *two* of the following extracts and (i)
Describe the scene presented as graphically as possible in your own words;
(ii) Comment on any features of the language employed which contribute to
the effect Crabbe has aimed to produce:

(*a*) . . . when the father in the Bible read
He in contempt and anger left the shed:
'It is the word of life', the parent cried:
– 'This is the life itself', the boy replied. (ll. 16–19)

(*b*) Pinned, beaten, cold, pinch'd, threaten'd and abused –
His efforts punish'd and his food refused, –
Awake tormented, – soon aroused from sleep, –
Struck if he wept, and yet compelled to weep,
The trembling boy dropp'd down and strove to pray. (ll. 79–83)

(c) Here dull and hopeless he'd lie down and trace
    How sidelong crabs had scrawled their crooked race;
    Or sadly listen to the tuneless cry
    Of fishing gull or clanging golden-eye;
    What time the sea birds to the marsh would come,
    And the loud bittern, from the bulrush home,
    Gave from the salt-ditch side the bellowing boom. (ll. 192–198)

There is nothing particularly sacrosanct about this set of questions, which are intended to prompt further thought and discussion, and possibly also further experiment. It will be noted that they make some use of the multiple-choice objective type of question, and it is of some interest to consider how this type of test (which takes some time to prepare but less time to check) can be developed for the testing of work in literature. On the other hand, many of the questions still require students to formulate their own individual answers, indicating the kinds of concept they have formed, and the kinds of appreciation they have made. Part i of Group 4 introduces a little-tried idea giving students the opportunity of revealing their responses to particular episodes or passages not by intellectual analysis but by creative writing.

The overriding consideration is the extent to which the type of test decided upon (a) encourages a close practical approach to the text throughout the period of study, (b) tests the student's personal capacity for genuine response. When tests fulfilling these conditions have been put into operation, examinations in literature will indicate students' real ability far more reliably than they do at present.

It is perhaps a pity to throw too much attention on to questions of testing and examination, for students and teachers tend to be too much preoccupied with them already. It has been a general theme of this chapter that as much of the stress as possible should be taken out of examinations. Amongst other things this means also that as much *irrelevance* as possible should also be removed. What is required of students for an examination should be nothing more than what is regarded as fundamental to their course of study *even if there were no examination to follow it*. If the values which are claimed in this book for the study of literature are to be preserved, the work must be undertaken above all for its own sake, and not for any ulterior motive. While we must still work to develop systems of education which encourage and reward the right kinds of approach to literature, there are still good grounds for supposing that even under existing systems, students who approach their work intelligently will receive due recognition.

Appendix A

SOME BOOKS FOR THE TEACHER OF LITERATURE

BRIGHT, J. A. and MCGREGOR, G. P.	*Teaching English as a Second Language* (especially chapters 3, 6 and 7)	Longman
ENGHOLM, S.	*Education through English*	C.U.P.
GRAHAM, D.	*Introduction to Poetry*	O.U.P.
GURREY, P.	*The Appreciation of Poetry*	O.U.P.
LEE, W. S. (ed.)	*English Language Teaching I and II*	O.U.P.
LERNER, L. D.	*English Literature: an Interpretation for Students Abroad*	O.U.P.
LUDOWYCK	*Understanding Shakespeare*	C.U.P.
MAYHEAD, R.	*Understanding Literature*	C.U.P.
MONFRIES, H.	*Literary Appreciation for Overseas Students*	Macmillan
MOODY, H. L. B.	*Literary Appreciation*	Longman
MOORE, G. H.	*African Literature and the Universities*	Ibadan University Press
PERREN, G.	*Teaching of English as a Second Language*	C.U.P.
PRESS, L. (ed.)	*The Teaching of English Literature Overseas*	Methuen
RAWLINSON, C.	*The Practice of Criticism*	C.U.P.
RICHARDS, I. A.	*Practical Criticism*	Routledge
STYAN, J. L.	*The Elements of Drama*	Cambridge

Appendix B

1 SECONDARY SCHOOLS: LITERATURE IN ENGLISH
A GRADED LIST

This list has been built up empirically: it was based in the initial stages on the actual reading lists used in a particular West African secondary school, and has been extended with suggestions made by experienced teachers from other areas. The list in general is related to the sequence observed in the series of graded readers published by some leading publishers, but many of the books recommended do not come from standard series. The main aim of the list is to show the range of reading materials available from many sources, and considerable importance has been attached to the interest and relevance of the contents of the books suggested.

For convenience of reference, the principal series from which selections have been made, and in which numerous other titles are available, are set out as follows:

Heinemann	Booster Books (Booster)
	African Writers Series (A.W.S.)
Longman New Method	Supplementary Readers (N.M.S.R.)
	Simplified English Series (S.E.S.)
	Lives of Achievement (L.A.)
	Bridge Series (B.S.)
Macmillan	Stories to Remember (S.R.)
	Simplified Stories (S.S.)
Oxford University Press	New Oxford Supplementary Readers (N.S.R.)
	Story Readers for Africa (S.R.A.)
	Stories Told and Retold (S.T.R.)
	Tales Retold for easy reading (T.R.)

YEAR 1

Prose

AKINSEMOYIN	*Twilight and the Tortoise*	African Universities Press (A.U.P.)
BENNETT, R.	*The Unexpected Christmas*	University of London Press (U.L.P.)
BERRY, A.	*The Pot of Gold*	Evans

CERVANTES	*Don Quixote*	Macmillan (Stories to Remember – S.R.)
CHALK, W. C. H.	*Escape from Bondage*	Heinemann (Booster Books)
CHALK, W. C. H.	*The Man from Mars*	Heinemann (Booster)
DOYLE, A. C.	*Stories of Sherlock Holmes*	Macmillan (S.R.)
DUMAS, A.	*Monte Cristo*	Longman (N.M.S.R. 3)
EKWENSI, C.	*The Great Elephant Bird*	Nelson
FAULKNER, J. M.	*Moonfleet*	Longman (N.M.S.R. 3)
FRAZER, S.	*The Crocodile Dies Twice*	Oxford University Press (O.U.P.)
FUJA, A.	*Fourteen Hundred Cowries*	O.U.P.
GREEN, M. (ed.)	*Tales from the Ramayan*	Macmillan (S.R.)
HARRIS, J.	*The Sleeping Mountain*	Longman (N.M.S.R. 3)
HERTSET, J.	*Mpala*	O.U.P. (Story Readers for Africa – S.R.A.)
HILTON, J.	*Lost Horizon*	Macmillan (S.R.)
HOYLE, D. J.	*Drums at Buntale*	Evans
JACKSON, H. V. (ed.)	*West African Folk Tales*, I	U.L.P.
KASTNER, E.	*Emil & The Detectives*	Longman (N.M.S.R. 3)
KAYE, G.	*Anan & The Grass Village*	O.U.P. (New Oxford Supplementary Readers) N.O.S.R. Grade 3A
KITCHENER and ETHERTON	*Malayan Jungle Adventures*	Longman
LEE, F. and F.	*Secret in Sabah*	O.U.P.
LEE, F.	*Time Out in Sabah*	O.U.P.
LOCKE	*The Tigers of Trenggam*	Harrap
MORSE, E.	*Chang*	Dent (Kings Treasuries)
MOWRY, I. M.	*Hoodt-Hoodt*	Longman (N.M.S.R. 2)
NZEKU and CROWDER	*Eze goes to School*	A.U.P.
RAO, R. (ed.)	*Tales of Ancient India*	Longman (N.M.S.R. 2)
RIDLEY, A.	*The Ghost Train*	Longman (N.M.S.R. 4)
SCHAEFER, J.	*Shane*	Heinemann
'SHANWA'	*The Chief's Shadow*	O.U.P. (S.R.A. 3)
'SHANWA'	*The Crocodile Man*	O.U.P. (New Supplementary Readers, 4)
SWIFT	*Gulliver's Travels, etc.*	Longman (N.M.S.R. 2)
TEDMAN, J. A.	*The Secret of the Castle*	O.U.P. (N.S.R. 4)
THORN	*The Adventures of Jonathan*	O.U.P.
TINGAY, F. J. F.	*Wing Ears*	O.U.P. (N.S.R. 4)
VALLERY	*Tales from the Heart of Africa*	U.L.P.
VERNE, J.	*From Earth to Moon*	Longman (N.M.S.R. 3)
WHYTE, R.	*Hamid's Holiday*	O.U.P. (N.S.R. 4)

WIMBUSH, D.	*The Kidnappers*	O.U.P.
WIMBUSH, D.	*The Land of the Crocodiles'* *Teeth*	O.U.P.
WIMBUSH, D.	*A Strange Adventure*	O.U.P.
WEST, M. (ed.)	*Tales from the Arabian Knights*	Longman (N.M.S.R. 2)
WYATT (ed.)	*The Tale of the 'Bounty'*	O.U.P. (Stories Told and Retold)
WYNDHAM J.	*The Midwich Cuckoos*	Longman (N.M.S.R. 3)
WYSS, J. R.	*The Swiss Family Robinson*	Macmillan (S.R.)

Poetry

BICKLEY, V. (ed.)	*Poems to Enjoy*, IV	U.L.P.
GRIEVE, D. W.	*Adventures into Poetry*	Macmillan
HALL, L.	*The Point of Poetry*	Nelson (Australia)
HANRATTY, J.	*The Wheel of Poetry*, Book I	U.L.P.
HERBERT (ed.)	*The Overseas Poetry*, Book II	Longman
MATHEW (ed.)	*Living Poetry*	Arnold
PINION, J. B.	*Shorter Narrative Poems*	Arnold
TAIWO, O.	*Collected Poems for Secondary Schools*	Macmillan

Plays

HSIUNG, S. I.	*Lady Precious Stream*	O.U.P.
LAURIE, R.	*Scenes and Ideas*	Evans
MORAN	*The Play Begins*	Cheshire (Melbourne)
ORR, A. R.	*Invitation to Drama*	Arnold
SHERIDAN, T. J.	*Four Short Plays*	O.U.P.
WALSH, J. R.	*Six One-Act Plays from Literature*	Longman

YEAR 2

Prose

ACHEBE, C.	*Chike and the River*	Cambridge University Press (C.U.P.)
AJOSE, A.	*Yomi's Adventure*	C.U.P.
AKPABOT, A.	*Sale and her Friends*	Nelson
BALLANTYNE, R. M.	*Coral Island*	Macmillan (S.R.)
BALLANTYNE, R. M.	*Martin Rattler*	Nelson; Macmillan (S.R.)
BERGSMA, H. and R.	*Tales Tiv Tell*	O.U.P.
BLACKMORE, R. D.	*Lorna Doone*	Longman (N.M.S.R. 4)
BROWNLEE and ROSS	*Commonwealth Short Stories*	Nelson
BUCHAN, J.	*The Power House*	Longman (S.E.S.)
BUDDEN, J.	*Jungle John*	Longman (N.M.S.R. 4)
CHALK, W. C. H.	*The Gomez Story*	Heinemann (Booster)
CLARKE, A. C.	*A Fall of Moondust*	Nelson

CLARKE, P. H. C.	*Adventures at Dabanga School*	Oxford University Press (Stories Told and Retold – S.T.R.)
DEFOE, D.	*Robinson Crusoe*	Macmillan (S.R.)
DELANO, I. O.	*Oba Ademola II*	O.U.P.
DICK, A. J. B.	*Milestones*	Nelson
DICKENS, C.	*Oliver Twist*	Macmillan (S.R.)
DICKENS, C.	*A Christmas Carol*	Longman (N.M.S.R. 5)
DODD, E. F. (ed.)	*Stories from Homer*	Macmillan (S.R.)
DODD, E. F. (ed.)	*Six Short Stories*	Macmillan (S.R.)
EKWENSI, C.	*An African Night's Entertainment*	A.U.P.
EKWENSI, C.	*The Drummer Boy*	C.U.P.
EKWENSI, C.	*The Passport of Malam Ilia*	C.U.P.
FORBES STUART	*Horned Animals Only*	Nelson
FORESTER, C. S.	*The 'African Queen'*	Longman (N.M.S.R. 4)
FORESTER, C. S.	*The Gun*	Longman (N.M.S.R. 5)
GANTHONY, R.	*A Message from Mars*	Longman (N.M.S.R. 5)
GOLDSMITH, O.	*The Vicar of Wakefield*	Macmillan (S.R.)
GREEN, M. (ed.)	*The Arabian Nights*	Macmillan (S.R.)
GREEN, M. (ed.)	*Wonder Tales from Greece*	Macmillan (S.R.)
GUILLOT, R.	*Kpo the Leopard*	Heinemann (N.W.S.)
HAGGARD, H. R.	*She*	Longman (N.M.S.R. 4)
HAGGARD, H. R.	*King Solomon's Mines*	Longman (N.M.S.R. 5)
HEYERDAHL, T.	*The Kon Tiki Expedition*	Longman (B.S.)
JACKSON, H. V. (ed.)	*West African Folk Tales*, II	U.L.P.
LEAVITT	*Great Men and Women*	Longman (N.M.S.R. 5)
LONDON, J.	*The Call of the Wild*	Longman (N.M.S.R. 4)
MAURIER, D. DU	*The Scapegoat*	Longman (N.M.S.R. 4)
MELVILLE, H.	*Typee*	Longman (N.M.S.R. 5)
MILSOME, J. R.	*El Kanemi*	O.U.P.
MUSSON, M.	*Pilgrimage for Two*	Nelson
NICOL, A.	*The Truly Married Woman and Other Stories*	O.U.P.
NWANKWO, N.	*Tales out of School*	A.U.P.
ODAGA, A.	*The Secret of Monty Rock*	Nelson
OLUGUNNA, O.	*The Story of Transport*	Evans
ONADIPO	*The Adventures of Souza*	A.U.P.
SABATINI, R.	*Captain Blood*	Macmillan (S.R.)
SCHAEFER, J.	*Old Ramon*	Heinemann (N.W.S.)
SHERIDAN, T. J. (ed.)	*Seven Chinese Stories*	O.U.P.
SHERRY, S.	*Street of the Small Night Market*	Cape
SIDAHOME, J. E.	*Stories of the Benin Empire*	O.U.P.
SIMMS, P. F. J.	*The Treasures of a Kingdom*	O.U.P. (S.T.R.)
SKINNER, E. and J.	*Haile Selassie: Lion of Judah*	Nelson

STANDING, T. G.	*African Explorers*	Longman (N.M.S.R. 4)
STEVENSON, R. L.	*Treasure Island*	Longman (N.M.S.R. 5)
SUGIMOTO	*A Daughter of the Samurai*	Hutchinson
TAGORE, R.	*Tales from Tagore*	Macmillan (S.R.)
TEDMAN, J. and A.	*Fire in the Forest*	O.U.P. (N.S.R. 5)
TEMPLE and SEKONI	*Kaunda of Zambia*	Nelson
VERNE, J.	*Round the World in Eighty Days*	Longman (S.E.S.)
VERNE, J.	*A Journey to the Centre of the Earth*	Longman (S.E.S.)
WARNER, R.	*Men and Gods*	Heinemann (N.W.S.)
WEAR, G. F. (ed.)	*Tales of Crime Detection*	O.U.P. (Tales Retold Γ.R.)
WEAR, G. F.	*Lost on Sinai*	O.U.P. (Tales Retold)
WELLS, H. G.	*The First Men in the Moon*	Longman (S.E.S.)
WELLS, H. G.	*The Time Machine*	Longman (N.M.S.R. 6)
YOUNGBERG, N. R.	*The Tiger of Lembal Pahit*	O.U.P.

Poetry

BERRY, A.	*Poetry for Africa*, II	U.L.P.
BICKLEY, V.	*Poems to Enjoy*, V	U.L.P.
EDWARDS, P. (ed.)	*A Ballad Book for Africa*	Nelson
HALL, L. (ed.)	*The Point of Poetry*, Book II	Nelson (Australia)
HANRATTY, J. (ed.)	*The Wheel of Poetry*, Book II	U.L.P.
HERBERT (ed.)	*The Overseas Poetry*, Book III	Longman
MATTHEW (ed.)	*Living Poetry*, Book II	Arnold
SUMMERFIELD, G.	*Voices*, I	Penguin
TONG, R.	*African Helicon*	Evans
TURNER	*Poetry for Overseas Students*	Harrap

Plays

BOOTH, P. J.	*Six One Act Plays for African Schools*	U.L.P.
BROOK, M.	*The Play for Yejide, etc.*	Heinemann
MCKELLAR, H. D. (ed.)	*Beyond the Footlights*	Arnold
OLAGOKE, D. O.	*The Incorruptible Judge*	Evans
WALSH (ed.)	*Nine One Act Plays*	Longman

YEAR 3

Prose

ABRAHAMS, P.	*Tell Freedom*	Allen & Unwin (Sch. edn.)
ABRUQUAH, J. W.	*The Catechist*	Allen & Unwin
ATTWOOD, E. M.	*Louis Pasteur*	Longman (L.A.)
BATES, H. E.	*The Jacaranda Tree*	Longman (S.E.S.)

BATES, H. E.	*The Purple Plain*	Nelson
BRAUMANN, F.	*Maliki and Amina*	O.U.P. (S.T.R.)
BROUGHTON, G. (ed.)	*Climbing Everest*	O.U.P. (English Readers Library)
BROUGHTON, G.	*The Splendid Tasks*	O.U.P. (E.R.L.)
BUCK, P.	*The Good Earth*	Longman (S.E.S.)
CANAWAY, W. H.	*The Ring Givers*	Longman (S.E.S.)
CARTER, M. E.	*Captain Scott*	Longman (L.A.)
CERVANTES, M. DE	*Don Quixote*	Macmillan (S.R.)
CHALK, W. C. H.	*The Secret Factory*	Heinemann (Booster)
COLLINS, W.	*The Moonstone*	Macmillan (S.R.)
CRONIN, A. J.	*The Citadel*	Longman (S.E.S.)
CURIE, E.	*Madame Curie*	Longman (L.A.)
DENNY, N. (ed.)	*Pan African Stories*	Nelson
DICK, J. (ed.)	*Eight Tales from Chaucer*	Nelson
DICKENS, C.	*A Tale of Two Cities*	Longman (S.E.S.)
DUMAS, A.	*The Three Musketeers*	Longman (S.E.S.)
DUMAS, A.	*The Count of Monte Cristo*	Macmillan (S.R.)
DURRELL, G.	*My Family and Other Animals*	Allen & Unwin
EDWARDS, P. (ed.)	*Modern African Narrative*	Nelson
EDWARDS, P. (ed.)	*Through African Eyes*	C.U.P.
EKWENSI, C.	*Trouble in Form Six*	C.U.P.
ELIOT, G.	*Silas Marner*	Longman (N.M.S.R. 6)
FORESTER, C. S.	*Flying Colours*	Longman (S.E.S.)
FRAZER	*A Time of Darkness*	O.U.P.
HAGGARD, H. R.	*Morning Star*	Longman (N.M.S.R. 6)
HIGHAM, C. S. S.	*Pioneers of Progress*	Longman (S.E.S.)
HOPE, A.	*The Prisoner of Zenda*	Longman (S.E.S.)
HOUSEHOLD, G.	*The Watcher in the Shadows*	Longman (S.E.S.)
HOWE, D. H.	*The Rain Makers*	O.U.P. (S.T.R.)
JOHNSTONE, A.	*Marco Polo*	Longman (L.A.)
KELLER, H.	*The Story of my Life*	Longman (L.A.)
KINGSLEY, C.	*Westward Ho*	Macmillan (S.R.)
LAYE, C.	*The African Child*	Collins
LYTTON, B.	*The Last Days of Pompeii*	Macmillan (S.R.)
MASEFIELD, J.	*Jim Davis*	Puffin
MAURIER, D. DU	*Rebecca*	Longman (S.E.S.)
MAURIER, D. DU	*Jamaica Inn*	Longman (S.E.S.)
MAXWELL	*In Malay Forests*	E.U.P.
NICOL, A.	*Two African Tales*	C.U.P.
ORCZY, BARONESS	*The Scarlet Pimpernel*	Macmillan (S.R.)
PINTO, O.	*Spy Catcher*	Nelson
POE, E. A.	*Tales of Mystery and Imagination*	Longman (S.E.S.)
RAMCHAND, K.	*West Indian Narrative*	Nelson
SCOTT, W.	*The Talisman*	Macmillan (S.R.)

SEBUKIMA, D.	*A Son of Kabira*	O.U.P. (East African Library)
SERRAILLIER, I.	*The Way of Danger*	Heinemann (N.W.S.)
SHERMAN, D. R.	*Old Mali and the Boy*	Heinemann (N.W.S.)
SHUTE, N.	*A Town like Alice*	Heinemann (N.W.S.)
SPERRY, A.	*The Boy who was Afraid*	Heinemann (N.W.S.)
STEVENS, S. F.	*Unlawful Cargo*	O.U.P. (S.T.R.)
STEVENSON, R. L.	*Dr. Jekyll and Mr. Hyde*	Longman (S.E.S.)
STEVENSON, R. L.	*Kidnapped*	Macmillan (S.R.)
TAGORE, R.	*More Tales from Tagore*	Macmillan (S.R.)
THORNLEY (ed.)	*British and American Short Stories*	Longman (S.E.S.)
VERNE, J.	*The Clipper of the Clouds*	Macmillan (S.R.)
WALTERS, J. G.	*African Triumph*	Allen & Unwin
WARNER	*Greeks and Trojans*	Heinemann (N.W.S.)
WASHINGTON, B. T.	*Up from Slavery*	Longman (L.A.)
WELLS, H. G.	*The Invisible Man*	Longman (S.E.S.)
WELLS, H. G.	*Bealby* (ed. Thornhill)	Methuen
WILLIAMS, E.	*The Wooden Horse*	Longman (S.E.S.)
WILSON, E.	*Coorina*	Longman (Heritage of Literature Series)
WYNDHAM, J.	*The Kraken Wakes*	Longman (S.E.S.)

Poetry

BEIER, U. (ed.)	*African Poetry*	C.U.P.
BERRY, A.	*Poetry for Africa*, III	U.L.P.
FIGUEROA, J.	*Caribbean Voices*, II	Evans
HEWETT, R. P.	*A Choice of Poets*	Harrap
O'MALLEY and THOMPSON	*Rhyme and Reason*	Chatto & Windus
PARSONS, D. ST. J.	*An Anthology of West African Verse*	U.L.P.
RULKA, C.	*An Anthology of Narrative Verse*	Macmillan
SUMMERFIELD, G.	*Voices*, II	Penguin
TAYLOR, W. E.	*The Poet and the Palm*	Arnold

Plays

BRAITHWAITE, E.	*Odale's Choice*	Evans
BRIGHT, J. A.	*Six Short Plays*	Longman
CHARLTON, J. N.	*Pan Book of One Act Plays*	Pan Books
COOK, D., LEE, M.	*Short East African Plays in English*	Heinemann
HENSHAWE, J. E.	*Children of the Goddess*	U.L.P.
HENSHAWE, J. E.	*This is our Chance*	U.L.P.
LADIPO, D.	*Three Plays*	Heinemann (A.W.S.)

| TAYLOR, R. V. (ed.) | *Shakespeare for Secondary Schools* | Macmillan |
| WOOD, M. | *Third Windmill Book of One Act Plays* | Heinemann |

YEAR 4

Prose

ABRAHAMS, P.	*Mine Boy*	Heinemann (A.W.S.)
ACHEBE, C.	*Things Fall Apart*	Heinemann (A.W.S.)
ACHEBE, C.	*No Longer at Ease*	Heinemann (A.W.S.)
ALUKO, T. M.	*One Man, One Matchet*	Heinemann (A.W.S.)
ALUKO, T. M.	*Kinsman and Foreman*	Heinemann (A.W.S.)
BENNETT, A.	*The Card*	Longman (B.S.)
BEST, H.	*The Road to Ticonderoga*	Penguin
BOULE, P.	*The Bridge on the River Kwai*	Heinemann (N.W.S.)
BRONTE, E.	*Wuthering Heights*	Macmillan (S.R.)
CALDWELL, J.	*Desperate Voyage*	Heinemann (N.W.S.)
CAREY, J.	*Mister Johnson*	Penguin
CLARK, J. P.	*America their America*	Heinemann (A.W.S.)
COLE, R. B.	*Kossoh Town Boy*	C.U.P.
CONTON, W.	*The African*	Heinemann (A.W.S.)
COOK, D. (ed.)	*Origin East Africa*	Heinemann (A.W.S.)
CRANE, S.	*The Red Badge of Courage*	Longman (B.S.)
DICKENS, C.	*A Tale of Two Cities*	Macmillan (S.R.)
DICKENS, C.	*Great Expectations*	Longman (B.S.)
DIOP, B.	*Tales of Amadou Koumba* (trans.)	O.U.P.
DOORLY, E.	*The Microbe Man*	Heinemann (N.W.S.)
DOORLY, E.	*The Radium Woman*	Heinemann (N.W.S.)
DURRELL, G.	*Encounters with Animals*	Heinemann (N.W.S.)
EASMON, S. R.	*The Burnt Out Marriage*	Nelson
ECKERSLEY, C. E. (ed.)	*England and the English*	Longman
EDWARDS, P.	*Equiano's Travels*	Heinemann (A.W.S.)
EKWENSI, C.	*Burning Grass*	Heinemann (A.W.S.)
EKWENSI, C.	*People of the City*	Heinemann (A.W.S.)
ELIOT, G.	*The Mill on the Floss*	Macmillan (S.R.)
FAGUNWA, D. O. (trans. Soyinka)	*The Forest of a Thousand Demons*	Nelson
GOLDING, W.	*Lord of the Flies*	Faber
HARDY, T.	*The Mayor of Casterbridge*	Macmillan (S.R.)
HEMINGWAY, E.	*The Old Man and the Sea*	Penguin
HEMMING, J.	*Mankind Against the Killer*	Longman (B.S.)
INNES, H.	*Campbell's Kingdom*	Longman (S.E.S.)
KONADU, A.	*A Woman in her Prime*	Heinemann (A.W.S.)

MCGRIFFIN, L.	*On the Trail to Sacramento*	Heinemann (N.W.S.)
MOFOLO, J.	*Chaka the Zulu*	O.U.P. (E.R.L.)
MORGAN, C.	*The River Line*	Macmillan (S.S.)
MPHAHLELE, E.	*Down Second Avenue*	Faber (Education)
MUNTHE, A.	*The Story of San Michele*	Murray (Sch. Edn.)
NAIPAUL, V. S.	*A House for Mr. Biswas*	Penguin
NAIPAUL, V. S.	*The Mystic Masseur*	Penguin
NEVILLE, C. J.	*Salifu the Detective*	Macmillan (Young Venture Library)
NGUGI, J.	*Weep Not Child*	Heinemann (A.W.S.)
NOYCE, W.	*South Col*	Heinemann (N.W.S.)
ORWELL, G.	*Animal Farm*	Penguin
OYONO, F.	*The Old Man and the Medal*	Heinemann (A.W.S.)
PATON, A.	*Cry the Beloved Country*	Penguin
POST, L. VAN DER	*The Lost World of the Kalahari*	Chatto & Windus
RIVE, R. (ed.)	*Modern African Prose*	Heinemann (A.W.S.)
SALEH, T.	*The Wedding of Zen*	Heinemann (A.W.S.)
SALKLEY, A. (ed.)	*Caribbean Prose*	Evans
SCOTT, W.	*Kenilworth*	Macmillan (S.R.)
SERRAILLIER, I.	*The Silver Sword*	Heinemann (N.W.S.)
'SHANWA'	*The Burning Star of Ndutu*	O.U.P. (S.R. 6)
SHUTE, N.	*No Highway*	Heinemann (New Windmill Series)
SNOW, C. P.	*The Masters*	Macmillan (S.S.)
STEINBECK, J.	*The Pearl*	Heinemann (N.W.S.)
TAGORE, R.	*Gora*	Macmillan (S.R.)
TAGORE, R.	*The Wreck*	Macmillan (S.R.)
TEDMAN, J. and A.	*The Battle of Valhome Dam*	O.U.P. (S.R. 6)
TWAIN, M.	*Huckleberry Finn*	Puffin
WHITE, S.	*Descent from the Hills*	Murray
WILLIAMS, J. H.	*Moshesh: the Man in the Mountain*	O.J.P. (E.R.L.)
WILLIAMS, J. G.	*Bandoola*	O.U.P. (E.R.L.)
WOUK, H.	*The Caine Mutiny*	Longman (B.S.)

Poetry

COGHILL, N.	*The Canterbury Tales* (translated)	Penguin
DICK, A. J. B.	*The Cambridge Book of Verse for African Schools*	C.U.P.
MILLER, D. C.	*A Choice of Poems*	O.U.P.
NWOGA, D. (ed.)	*West African Verse*	Longman
REED, J. and WAKE, C.	*A Book of African Verse*	Heinemann (A.W.S.)
SERGEANT, H.	*New Voices of the Commonwealth*	Evans

SERGEANT, H. (ed.)	*Poetry from Africa* (Okara, Bart-Williams, Brew and Rubadiri)	Pergamon Press (Pergamon Poets II)
SUMMERFIELD, G.	*Voices,* III	Penguin
TAIWO, O.	*Collected Poems for Secondary Schools*	Macmillan
UNTERMEYER, L.	*Albatross Book of Living Verse*	Collins
VARIOUS	*Poems from Singapore*	Poetry Singapore
WILLIAMS, G. A.	*Poems from Ghana*	Heinemann (A.W.S.)

Plays

EASMON, S. R.	*Dear Parent and Ogre*	O.U.P.
EGBUNA, O. B.	*The Anthill*	O.U.P.
HENSHAWE, J. E.	*Dinner for Promotion*	U.L.P.
HUTCHINSON, A.	*The Rain Killers*	U.L.P.
IBSEN, H.	*An Enemy of the People*	Heinemann (Drama Library)
IJIMERE, O.	*The Imprisonment of Obatala*	Heinemann (A.W.S.)
MACLEISH, K. (ed.)	*Four Greek Plays*	Longman
NGUGI, J.	*The Black Hermit*	Heinemann (A.W.S.)
NKOSI, L.	*The Rhythm of Violence*	O.U.P.
PIERTESEE, C. (ed.)	*Ten One Act Plays*	Heinemann (A.W.S.)
PRIESTLEY, J. B.	*An Inspector Calls*	Heinemann
RATTIGAN, T.	*The Winslow Boy*	Longman
SHAKESPEARE, W.	*Julius Caesar, Macbeth, etc.*	Longman (New Swan Edn.)
SHAW, G. B.	*Saint Joan*	Penguin
WEAR, G. F. (ed.)	*Three One Act Plays*	Longman
WILDER, T.	*Our Town*	Longman

2 FURTHER SUGGESTIONS FOR READING IN POST SCHOOL CERTIFICATE CLASSES

ABRAHAMS, P.	*Wreath for Udomo*	Faber
ACHEBE, C.	*Arrow of God*	Heinemann
ALLINGHAM, M.	*Tiger in the Smoke*	Heinemann
ALUKO, T. M.	*One Man One Wife*	Heinemann
AMIS, K.	*Lucky Jim*	Penguin
ANTHONY, M.	*The Games were coming*	Deutsch
ASALACHE, K.	*A Calabash of Life*	Longman
BALLARD, J. G.	*The Drought*	Penguin
BALZAC, E.	*Old Goriot*	Penguin
BARSTOW, S.	*A Kind of Loving*	Penguin
BARSTOW, S.	*The Human Element*	Longman
BATES, H. E.	*Fair Stood the Wind for France*	Penguin

BELLOW, S.	*Herzog*	Penguin
BELLOW, S.	*Henderson the Rain King*	Penguin
BENNETT, A.	*Anna of the Five Towns*	Penguin
BERGER, J.	*A Fortunate Man*	Penguin
BRADBURY, R.	*The Day it Rained Forever*	Penguin
BRAINE, J.	*Room at the Top*	Penguin
BRÖNTE, C.	*Jane Eyre*	Penguin
BRÖNTE, E.	*Wuthering Heights*	Penguin
BUTLER, S.	*The Way of all Flesh*	Penguin
BUTLER, S.	*Erewhon*	Dent
CAMUS, A.	*The Plague*	Penguin
CAREY, J.	*Mister Johnson*	Penguin
CAREY, J.	*The Horse's Mouth*	Pergamon
CAREY, J.	*Aissa Saved*	Pergamon
CHANDLER, R.	*The Big Sleep*	Penguin
CHANDLER, R.	*Farewell my Lovely*	Penguin
CHAPLIN	*My Autobiography*	Penguin
CHESTERTON, G. K.	*The Innocence of Father Brown*	Penguin
CHESTERTON, G. K.	*The Man who was Thursday*	Penguin
CHRISTOPHER, J.	*The Death of Grass*	Pergamon
CLOSTERMAN, P.	*The Big Show*	Chatto & Windus
DAVIDSON, B.	*Old Africa Rediscovered*	Gollancz
DEIGHTON, L.	*The Billion Dollar Brain*	Penguin
DICKENS, C.	*Bleak House*	Penguin
DICKENS, C.	*Hard Times*	Penguin
DICKENS, C.	*Martin Chuzzlewit*	Penguin
DICKENS, M.	*One Pair of Hands*	Penguin
DIQS, I.	*A Bedouin Childhood*	Pergamon
DONLEAVY, J. P.	*The Ginger Man*	Penguin
DOS PASSOS, J.	*U.S.A.*	Penguin
DOSTOEVSKY, F.	*Crime and Punishment*	Penguin
DRABBLE, M.	*The Garrick Years*	Penguin
DREISER, T.	*Sister Carrie*	Oxford
DUODO, C.	*The Gab Boys*	Deutsch
DURRELL, G	*Bafut Beagles*	Penguin
DURRELL, G.	*My Family and other Animals*	Penguin
EKWENSI, C.	*Iska*	Hutchinson
FITZGERALD, F. S.	*The Great Gatsby*	Penguin
FLAUBERT, G.	*Madame Bovary*	Penguin
FORESTER, C. S.	*The Ship*	Penguin
FORESTER, C. S.	*Lord Hornblower*	Penguin
FORSTER, E. M.	*Room with a View*	Penguin
FORSTER, E. M.	*A Passage to India*	Penguin
FORSTER, E. M.	*Abinger Harvest*	Penguin
FORSTER, E. M.	*Two Cheers for Democracy*	Penguin
GALSWORTHY, J.	*A Man of Property*	Penguin

GOGOL, N.	*Dead Souls*	Oxford
GORDIMER, N.	*World of Strangers*	Penguin
GORKY, M.	*My Childhood*	Penguin
GRAVES, R.	*I, Claudius*	Penguin
GRAVES, R.	*Goodbye to All That*	Penguin
GREENE, G.	*The Brighton Rock*	Penguin
GREENE, G.	*A Burnt out Case*	Penguin
GREENE, G.	*The Comedians*	Penguin
GREENE, G.	*The Heart of the Matter*	Heinemann
GREENE, G.	*Our Man in Havana*	Heinemann
GREENE, G.	*The Ministry of Fear*	Penguin
GREENE, G.	*The Quiet American*	Penguin
GREENE, G.	*The Power and the Glory*	Penguin
HARRIS, W.	*Palace of the Peacock*	Faber
HARTLEY, L. P.	*The Go Between*	Penguin
HAWTHORNE, N.	*The Scarlet Letter*	Oxford
HEARNE, J.	*Stranger at the Gate*	Faber
HEMINGWAY, E.	*A Farewell to Arms*	Penguin
HEMINGWAY, A.	*For Whom the Bell Tolls*	Penguin
HOGGART, R.	*The Uses of Literacy*	Penguin
HOYLE, F.	*The Black Cloud*	Penguin
HUGHES, R.	*High Wind in Jamaica*	Penguin
HUGHES, R.	*In Hazard*	Penguin
HUXLEY, A.	*Chrome Yellow*	Penguin
HUXLEY, A.	*Antic Hay*	Penguin
HUXLEY, A.	*Brave New World*	Penguin
HUXLEY, E.	*The Merry Hippo*	Penguin
HUXLEY, E.	*The Flame Trees of Thika*	Penguin
IKE, C.	*Toads for Supper*	Collins
INNES, M.	*Appleby on Ararat*	Penguin
INNES, M.	*Death at the President's Lodging*	Penguin
JACOBSON, D.	*The Price of Diamonds*	Penguin
JAMES, H.	*The Europeans*	Penguin
JAMES, H.	*Portrait of a Lady*	Oxford
JEROME, J. K.	*Three Men in a Boat*	Penguin
JOYCE, J.	*Portrait of the Artist*	Heinemann
KAKKA, F.	*The Trial*	Penguin
KAMM, J.	*Out of Step*	Heinemann
KIRKUP	*The Only Child*	Pergamon
KNOX, R.	*The Three Taps*	Penguin
KOESTLER, A.	*Darkness at Noon*	Penguin
LAMMING, G.	*Season of Adventure*	Joseph
LAMMING, G.	*Pleasures of Exile*	Hutchinson
LAWRENCE, D. H.	*Sons and Lovers*	Penguin
LAWRENCE, D. H.	*The Rainbow*	Penguin
LAWRENCE, D. H.	*The Lost Girl*	Penguin

LAYE, C.	*A Dream of Africa*	Collins
LEE, H.	*To Kill a Mocking Bird*	Heinemann
LENNON, J.	*Penguin John Lennon*	Penguin
LERMONTOV	*A Hero of Our Time*	Oxford
LESSING, D.	*The Grass is Singing*	Joseph
LESSING, D.	*The Children of Violence*	McGibbon & Kee
LUTHULI, A.	*Let My People Go*	Collins
MACINNES, C.	*City of Spades*	Penguin
MACINNES, C.	*Absolute Beginners*	Penguin
MARLAND, M. (ed.)	*The Experience of Colour*	Longman
MASEFIELD, J.	*Sard Harker*	Penguin
MASTERS, J.	*Bowani Junction*	Penguin
MASTERS, J.	*Fandango Rock*	Penguin
MAUGHAM, S.	*Cakes and Ale*	Heinemann
MAUGHAM, S.	*Of Human Bondage*	Penguin
MAUGHAM, S.	*Ashenden*	Heinemann
MAUPASSANT, G.	*A Woman's Life*	Penguin
MAURIER, D. DU	*Frenchman's Creek*	Penguin
MAURIER, D. DU	*Jamaica Inn*	Penguin
MAURIER, D. DU	*Rebecca*	Penguin
MELVILLE, H.	*Billy Budd, Sailor, etc.*	Penguin
MELVILLE, H.	*Moby Dick*	Oxford
MIKES, G.	*How to be an Alien*	Penguin
MIKES, G.	*How to Unite Nations*	Penguin
MILL, J. S.	*Autobiography*	Oxford
MONSARRATT, N.	*The Cruel Sea*	Penguin
MURDOCH, I.	*The Bell*	Penguin
NAIPAUL, V. S.	*The Mimic Men*	Penguin
NAIPAUL, V. S.	*House for Mr. Biswas*	Penguin
NWAPA, F.	*Efuru*	Heinemann
NZEKWU, O.	*Blade Among the Boys*	Hutchinson
O'CONNOR, F.	*My Oedipus Complex, etc.*	Penguin
ORWELL, G.	*Burmese Days*	Heinemann
ORWELL, G.	*Keep the Aspidistra Flying*	Penguin
ORWELL, G.	*Nineteen Eighty Four*	Penguin
ORWELL, G.	*Down and Out in Paris and London*	Penguin
ORWELL, G.	*Coming up for Air*	Heinemann
PETERS, L.	*The Second Round*	Heinemann
PHELPS, G.	*The Winter People*	Penguin
POE, E. A.	*Selected Writings*	Penguin
POTTER, S.	*The Theory and Practice of Games-manship*	Penguin
PRIESTLEY, J. B.	*The Good Companions*	Penguin
ROLFE, F.	*Hadrian the Seventh*	
SALINGER, J. D.	*Catcher in the Rye*	Penguin
SARTRE, J. P.	*Words*	Penguin

SAYERS, D.	*Busman's Honeymoon*	Penguin
SAYERS, D.	*Have His Carcase*	Penguin
SELORMEY, F.	*The Narrow Path*	Heinemann
SHOLOKHOV, M.	*Fierce and Gentle Warriors*	Heinemann
SHUTE, N.	*An Old Captivity*	Heinemann
SIGAL, C.	*A Weekend in Dinlock*	Penguin
SIMENON, G.	*Black Rain*	Penguin
SIMENON, G.	*Madame Maigret's Find*	Penguin
SIMENON, G.	*Stain on the Snow*	Penguin
SINCLAIR, U.	*The Jungle*	Penguin
SNOW, C. P.	*Corridors of Power*	Penguin
SNOW, C. P.	*The Masters*	Penguin
SNOW, C. P.	*The New Men*	Penguin
SOYINKA, W.	*The Interpreters*	Deutsch
SPARK, M.	*Memento Mori*	Penguin
SPARK, M.	*The Go Away Bird*	Penguin
STAPLEDON, O.	*First and Last Men*	Penguin
STEINBECK, J.	*Grapes of Wrath*	Heinemann
STEINBECK, J.	*Of Mice and Men*	Penguin
STERNE, L.	*Sentimental Journey*	Penguin
THURBER, J.	*The Years with Ross*	Penguin
THURBER, J.	*Thurber Carnival*	Penguin
TOLSTOI, L.	*Anna Karenina*	Penguin
TOLSTOI, L.	*War and Peace*	Penguin
TROLLOPE, A.	*Barchester Towers*	Dent
TUTUOLA, A.	*Ajaye and his Inherited Poverty*	Faber
UPDIKE, J.	*The Centaur*	Penguin
UPDIKE, J.	*Of the Farm*	Penguin
UZONDINMA, E.	*Our Dead Speak*	Longman
VAN DER POST, L.	*Flamingo Feather*	Chatto & Windus
VAN DER POST, L.	*Lost World of the Kalarahi*	Chatto & Windus
VAN DER POST, L.	*The Heart of the Hunter*	Chatto & Windus
WAIN, J.	*Hurry on Down*	Penguin
WAIN, J.	*Strike the Father Dead*	Penguin
WATERHOUSE, K.	*Billy Liar*	Penguin
WATTS, J. (ed.)	*Encounters*	Longman
WAUGH, E.	*Black Mischief*	Penguin
WAUGH, E.	*The Loved One*	Heinemann
WAUGH, E.	*Scoop*	Penguin
WELLS, H. G.	*The War in the Air*	Penguin
WELLS, H. G.	*The War of the Worlds*	Penguin
WELLS, H. G.	*The Time Machine*	Heinemann
WHITE, P.	*Voss*	Penguin
WHITE, P.	*The Tree of Man*	Penguin
WHITE, T. H.	*The Once and Future King*	Cape
WHITE, T. H.	*Mistress Masham's Repose*	Penguin

WILDER, T.	*The Bridge of Sans Luis Rey*	Penguin
WILLIAMS, J. H.	*Elephant Bill*	Penguin
WILSON, A.	*Anglo-Saxon Attitudes*	Penguin
WILSON, A.	*Hemlock and After*	Penguin
WODEHOUSE, P. G.	*Carry on, Jeeves*	Penguin
WOOLF, V.	*Mrs. Dalloway*	Penguin
WOOLF, V.	*To the Lighthouse*	Penguin
WRIGHT, R.	*Black Boy*	Longman
WYNDHAM, J.	*Day of the Tryffyds*	Penguin
WYNDHAM, J.	*The Kraken Wakes*	Penguin